The Developing Child

Recent decades have witnessed unprecedented advances in research on human development. Each book in The Developing Child series reflects the importance of this research as a resource for enhancing children's well-being. It is the purpose of the series to make this resource available to that increasingly large number of people who are responsible for raising a new generation. We hope that these books will provide rich and useful information for parents, educators, child-care professionals, students of developmental psychology, and all others concerned with childhood.

Jerome Bruner, New School for Social Research
Michael Cole, University of California, San Diego
Barbara Lloyd, University of Sussex
Series Editors

The Developing Child Series

Daycare

Alison Clarke-Stewart

Harvard University Press
Cambridge, Massachusetts
1982

Library of Congress Cataloging in Publication Data
Clarke-Stewart, Alison, 1943–
    Daycare.

    (The Developing child)
    Bibliography: p.
    Includes index.
    1. Day care centers.   2. Child development.
I. Title.   II. Series.
HV851.C55   362.7'12   82-956
ISBN 0-674-19403-9   AACR2
ISBN 0-674-19404-7 (pbk.)

To Christopher,
who spent his first year in daycare
so that this book could be written

Acknowledgments

Although this book is based on my reading of all the available research reports relating to daycare, it was especially influenced by the process and results of my own research in this area (The Chicago Study of Child Care and Development). Among the students who spent long hours collecting and coding data for me, I am particularly grateful to Linda Fitzgerald, Margaret Ellis Snow, Linda Espinosa, Julie Spielberger, Harry Piotrowski, Kathy Cornell, Bonnie Umeh, Laima Vanderstoep, Connie Hevey, Lynn Barker, Janna Dresden, Carol Finder, Richard Rogers, Barbara Luskin, Miriam Rabban, Anita Wolfe, Jeffrey Rosenberg, Susan Giannino, Carol Draeger, Saba Ayman-Nolley, Katina Kay, and Terri Chappell. The Bush Foundation supported the data collection phase of the research, and the Spencer Foundation and the Foundation for Child Development helped in funding the data analyses. These people have added much to our knowledge about daycare and its effects on the development of young children, and I am grateful to them all.

Contents

Credits

All photographs were supplied by Stock/Boston.

The
Developing
Child

Daycare

1 / The Problem

"I don't know how you do it—the house, the kids, your job," the man in the television commercial admiringly comments to his wife. "I eat right, get plenty of rest, and take Geritol every day," she lovingly explains.

But most working mothers find it takes more than Geritol to accomplish the herculean task of balancing home, work, and family. Research shows that fulltime working mothers, on the average, spend forty hours a week on the job and another thirty-six hours on home and children.[1] This gives them two fulltime jobs. They may do less housework or they may complete their household chores in less time than they would if they were not working. They may plan and schedule their activities more rigorously. But they still spend about the same amount of time taking care of their children as they would if they were not employed. The tasks of bathing, feeding, dressing, teaching, and transporting the children do not disappear. Although husbands of married women who hold fulltime jobs are likely to help with the housework and children, there is no equal sharing of tasks between spouses. The primary responsibility and time commitment in most families is still the wife's, and even if she has hired help to assist with these tasks—a cleaning person, babysitter, housekeeper, laundry service—it is

1

still her responsibility to arrange for and manage such assistance. Three quarters of the mothers who are employed in fulltime jobs claim they don't have enough time to do everything. They cope with the situation by giving up time for themselves, spending significantly less time than nonworking mothers on hobbies, reading, gardening, partying, and other personal pleasures. And there seems to be no free time at all.

This double position of homemaker and jobtaker is further reflected in the physical and psychological condition of the working mother.[2] As a result of their constant efforts to juggle the demands of family and job, most mothers holding fulltime jobs feel tired and overworked. Many feel lonely and socially isolated, and all feel harried. There are compensations, of course. They feel good about getting out into the world and having new experiences. They get more satisfaction from their work than nonworking women do from housework. They feel better about themselves as individuals and as competent achievers. They feel healthier. They feel more independent and in control of their own lives. But they also feel rushed, tied down, and under pressure, especially when they are first adjusting to their dual role. Nor do they feel as good about themselves as mothers. Although they claim to be less vested in their maternal role than nonworking mothers, they worry more about the time spent with their children and feel guilty about leaving them when they have to go to work. They feel deprived of their children's company.

In light of these reported feelings, it has been suggested that, for mothers of preschool children, the dominant role is that of mother, and only if the demands of this role are met can a woman gain satisfaction from her other role as worker. If she is not satisfied with both roles, this is reflected not only in her own well-being but in her behavior with her child.* Dissatisfied women have been found to be less involved, affectionate, playful, stimulating, and effective with their children.[3]

For the working mother one of the most important contributions to satisfaction is what kind of arrangement is made for the care and supervision of the children while she is at work. If a mother cannot be assured that her children are safe in her absence, she can neither concentrate on her work nor feel she is doing right by her family. Only a small minority of the mothers who work are able to coordinate their schedules with their husbands' so that the father can take care of the children in their absence. The rest must make some other arrangement—with a relative, a housekeeper, a babysitter or childminder, a nursery school or daycare center. It is critical for each of these mothers, and their children, that a satisfactory daycare arrangement be made.

But this is not easy. For one thing, it is difficult to know what care arrangement to make because of the wide variety of types that are possible. Daycare may occur in the child's home or someone else's, in a home setting or a center, with an unpaid relative or a paid babysitter, with a friendly neighbor or a professional caregiver, with one other child or many, in a facility run by church, community organization, government, or school, in a program that stresses education, social skills, or play. How can a parent know what type of arrangement is most likely to be satisfactory?

---

* In this book I usually use the feminine *she/her* to refer to the parent or caregiver (since it is mothers and female caregivers who are the most relevant adults in discussions of daycare) and, therefore, to keep pronouns distinct, when necessary I use *he/his* to refer to an infant or child.

It is also difficult to arrange for daycare because of the enormous differences in the quality of care offered in each of these arrangements. The quality ranges from mere "custodial" care with minimal standards of safety and no program of stimulation to "developmental" care with frequent and fond attention from adult caregivers, a safe and interesting physical environment, the opportunity to play with other children, and a program of enriching educational experiences. Most daycare falls somewhere in between. How can a parent assess what is likely to be a high-quality daycare arrangement?

The third reason that arranging child care is hard is that, although these types and kinds of care are available nationwide, not all are available to every mother. Each mother has to make do with what she can find in her community or neighborhood, within her budget, fitting her schedule, and open to her child. A mother has to find a satisfactory daycare arrangement that meets her particular needs.

Another thing that makes arranging for daycare difficult is that "expert opinion" on the subject is divided. Child development authorities offer parents little guidance in making decisions about daycare. Some pediatricians, politicians, child psychologists, teachers, and clergymen are enthusiastic about the possibilities daycare offers mothers and children; others, equally eminent, are adamantly opposed to any nonparental childrearing. Some personal advisers (say feminist friends) are likely to endorse daycare; others, just as insistent (say mothers-in-law), are critical of it and of a mother's desire to work. This lack of consensus underscores the other daycare dilemmas and provides no constructive solutions to a mother's search for a good childcare arrangement.

Finally, the whole notion of daycare goes against the

traditional views of family and childrearing that our society has espoused for generations, family-oriented views that dominated the upbringing of most of today's working mothers themselves. The young working mother cannot fall back on traditional values or on her own childhood experiences for guidance. She must make decisions about daycare on her own, without expert or societal guidance, without full knowledge of what types of daycare are available and will prove most satisfactory, choosing from a limited set of options, each of unknown quality.

But daycare is a reality and a necessity for many millions of families right now, despite all the problems. It was with the aim of helping working and would-be working mothers solve some of the problems of arranging for satisfactory daycare that this book was written. It does not solve the problems, for there are no simple or universal solutions to those. Solutions depend on individual children, individual settings, and individual circumstances. But it does offer information that, I hope, will guide parents in solving the problems on their own.

It does this in several ways. One way is by describing the range of different kinds of daycare that are currently in use in the United States, Canada, and Great Britain. A second way is by reporting the results of research on the effects of these kinds of care on children's intellectual, social, and emotional development. A third way is by giving some information about what aspects of the daycare arrangement seem to accelerate or enhance chidren's development, such as the number of children in the daycare setting and their ages, the kind of equipment, the content of the program or curriculum, and the quality and training of the caregivers. The fourth way is by giving some hints about what kinds of daycare might be most suitable for individual children. And the final way is by offering some guidelines for finding and recognizing daycare settings of high quality.

But the problems of daycare go beyond individual parents and children. Providing facilities to support working mothers and their children is at least in part a responsibility of the society at large. For this reason the book also discusses the problem of daycare at the national level. It describes the current acute need for daycare in the United States and Great Britain, a need that far exceeds availability, and discusses this in the context of political, economic, and ideological forces that are responsible for the daycare shortage. It also documents by a brief history of daycare in the United States and Great Britain how daycare availability and use have always been linked to broader social issues. And finally, to broaden thinking about daycare even further to include consideration of potential options and to illustrate that there is no one simple solution to the problem at the national level either, a few of the ways that other nations are solving their daycare problems are described. All of these kinds of information should help readers understand the larger issues surrounding daycare and perhaps encourage them to support constructive social change that would reduce daycare problems for future generations.

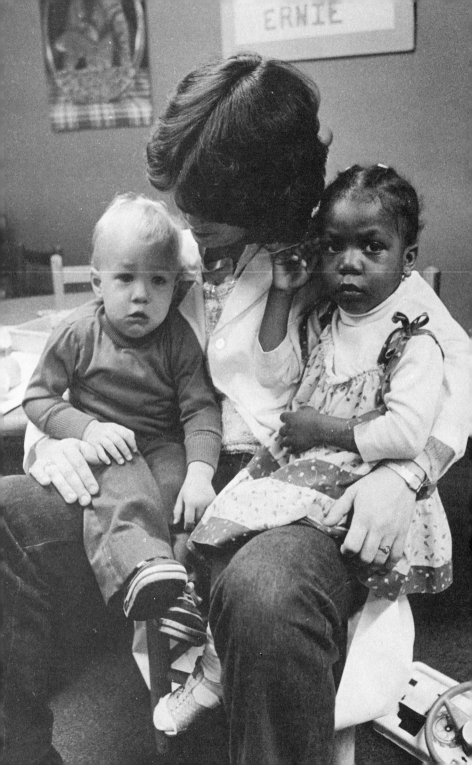

2 / New Needs

A number of social changes have affected the modern family and created a new need for daycare, a need more pressing than has ever existed before. Nonetheless, daycare facilities have not expanded to fill this need. It is important to find out why.

WORKING WOMEN

The major social change affecting the care of children has been the dramatic increase in the number of women who are employed in jobs outside the home. This trend has become almost a revolutionary tide in the past fifteen years. Now, for the first time, a majority of school-age children have mothers who work. Maternal employment is becoming the usual pattern, and the first question upon meeting a woman at a dinner party is often not "How do you do?" but "What do you do?" The fastest-growing group in the labor market is mothers of preschool children, particularly children under three. This trend is pronounced and worldwide. In Sweden, for example, we find a striking demonstration of the trend in the fact that the proportion of mothers of children under three who work has risen from one third to two thirds over the last decade. In the United States and the United Kingdom, the

Table 1. Percentage of Working Mothers of Preschool Children

| | Year | | | |
Country	1965	1970	1975	1980
United States	20	29	39	42
United Kingdom	14	19	26	29

In the U.S. more than two thirds of these women work fulltime; in the U.K. about one quarter work fulltime. U.S. statistics are for children under six; U.K. statistics are for children under five. Since the percentage of working mothers increases with the age of the child, U.K. and U.S. percentages are probably closer than the figures indicate. Statistics are from the U.S. Department of Labor and the U.K. Office of Population Censuses and Surveys.

proportion of working mothers of preschool children has doubled since the mid 1960s (see Table 1), and it is expected that this increase will continue, with some tapering off, until at least the end of this century.[1]

What has caused this dramatic rise in maternal employment? The primary and most obvious cause is economic. The desire to maintain or improve the family's standard of living, coupled with rising costs and high inflation, has led to a need for increased income in most families. In all surveys, the most common reason mothers give for working is, quite simply, that they need the money. Nevertheless, although financial needs may be foremost, there are other reasons. In one survey by the United States Department of Labor, 69 percent of the employed wives interviewed said they work for money, but 55 percent said they would continue to work even if they didn't need to.[2] A survey in Great Britain had a similar result: fewer than one fifth of the working mothers interviewed said they would stop working even if there were no financial need to work.[3]

Employed mothers also work because they like their jobs, because they want to have careers, because they want to get out of the house and meet people, have new experiences, avoid boredom, loneliness, or frustration—and because the "Women's Movement" of the 1960s and 1970s has made it easier for them to work. The Women's Movement contributed to the increase of working mothers by bringing pressure against job discrimination, by encouraging new employment and educational opportunities for women, and by making it fashionable to be a working woman. Women's Liberation replaced the traditional feminine mystique that "motherhood is fulfillment" with a radical feminist mystique that highlighted one question for women: "Am I fulfilling my potential for achievement in the real world?" Feminism encouraged women to be meaningfully employed and made many feel guilty if they "only" stayed at home doing housework and raising children. Many of these women's husbands, also influenced by the feminist viewpoint and not wanting to be accused of male chauvinism, urged their wives to work. A Department of Labor Dictionary of Occupational Titles, which ranks 22,000 occupations according to the complexity of skills each requires, illustrates an even more general devaluation of housework and childcare in American society. It places homemaker at the lowest level, along with restroom attendant, parking-lot attendant, and poultry-offal shoveler. If this is the attitude society holds, no wonder more and more women feel the need to escape the drudgery of being only housewives.

DIVORCE AND SINGLE PARENTHOOD

A second social trend that has ramifications for the daily care of children is the increase in family dissolution through divorce. Since the turn of the century, there has been a 700 percent rise in the number of marriages ending in divorce. Marriages are becoming like automobiles—short-lived and replaceable, with divorce an easy solution to an unsatisfactory marriage. Today in the United States, one third of all marriages end in divorce, and Great Britain and Canada are moving toward that figure. Every year in America, there are 800,000 divorces, affecting one million children. It is estimated that four out of ten children born in the 1970s will spend some time in a one-parent family. Like the increase in maternal employment, this trend is most striking for families with young children: the divorce rate for parents of preschool children has risen from 7 percent in 1948 to 18 percent in 1978. Even though the remarriage rate has kept pace with the divorce rate (nine out of ten divorced women remarry), between marriages a divorced mother usually lives alone with her children and works fulltime. And even when she remarries, she is likely to continue to work.

There has also been an increase in the number of unmarried women having and keeping their children. These women face the same difficulties of lone parenthood as divorced women. Whether divorced or never married, a single mother is more likely to live alone and to be employed. In the United States, a recent survey found that 56 percent of the single mothers of preschoolers work (more than 80 percent of them full-time) as against 33 percent of married mothers.[4]

PARTICIPATION OF FATHERS

Another social change that has affected contemporary child care is the increasingly active role fathers are taking in the care of their children. In many families, especially the more affluent ones, the father spends more time around the house than would or could have been possible a generation ago. This is so because of shorter working hours and less physically demanding work for men. Women's groups and the popular media also actively urge active participation by fathers in childcare. And in families where mothers have fulltime jobs and the parents share attitudes about equal roles for men and women, fathers have been found to be more involved in day-to-day childcare than they would have twenty years ago.[5] Fathers now are more likely to get involved with their children right from the beginning, with attendance at prenatal classes and the infant's birth. They are also more likely to ask for and get child custody in divorce cases and to be accepted as single adoptive parents.

One might expect, then, that this increase in paternal participation in childcare would compensate for the decreased availability of care by working mothers. Not so. In almost all families, childcare is still considered the mother's responsibility. At best, in most families the husband contributes a couple of hours a day to the running of the household. A report of four surveys just completed by several American advertising agencies confirms that, while married men readily endorse the idea of equal housework, they are slow to carry out anything more than the garbage.[6] While 60 percent of the 700 husbands surveyed voiced support for shared household responsibility, only 27 percent vacuumed and 29 percent helped with the laundry. One recent study asked parents to rate 89 childrearing activities in terms of ideal maternal and paternal responsibility.[7] Half of the activities were considered by these parents to be the mother's exclusive responsibility. (These included all physical caregiving, behavioral training, and aesthetic enrichment.) One third, having to do with education and discipline, could be shared and only eight activities, fewer than 10 percent, were considered to be the father's responsibility. (These involved guidance in traditionally masculine areas such as physical assertiveness, mechanical skills, and sports.)

This study no doubt reflects both current beliefs about appropriate roles for men and women and the realities of the fathers' available time. Working fathers, like working mothers, have limited time available for childcare and household tasks. The clearest predictor of the amount of time a father is likely to contribute to childcare is his work schedule, not his wife's. If the father works more than forty hours a week, he spends on the average about two hours a day on all kinds of household tasks, but if he works over fifty hours a week, he typically spends only one hour on housework and childcare.[8] Fathers, too, are victims of the economic pressures of inflation and increased expectations about standard of living, and though there has been some effort to promote a twenty-five hour work week for women—for example, by the New York employment firm New Time that advertises, "If Mme. Curie were alive today and only able to work from 9:30 to 3:15, would you hire her?"—there has been no such effort for fathers.

One compromise, "flexitime," has been suggested as a possible way of freeing working parents—both fathers and mothers—for childcare. In the flexitime system employees are required to maintain certain core hours at the job, but they can arrive or depart within a range of hours. Married couples can maximize the time one or the other of them can be home with their children, so they will not need to use as much daycare. Unfortunately, the most comprehensive study to date of the impact of this system on family life finds that, after a year of flexitime, male/female roles have not changed: childcare is still the mothers' responsibility; fathers still have work as their top priority.[9] Neither mothers nor fathers in this study reported spending more time with their children than workers in a comparable office on regular schedules. As one father said, "Work makes clear objective calls on you, and the penalties if you don't meet them are explicit and obvious. The demands, requests, and pleas from your family are not. That tends to tilt the balance toward work."

Another compromise that has been offered in some countries is the paternity leave, a leave of absence from the job for several months after the birth of a baby. Here again, no marked change has resulted; few fathers take advantage of the leave.

At least at the present, then, despite wishful thinking, in most families there is still a need for daily care beyond what the parents alone can provide.

SMALLER FAMILIES

One further social change that has affected the need for childcare is the decreasing availability of other relatives such as grandparents, older siblings, and aunts. The trend toward smaller families in Western countries has both immediate and long-range implications for childcare. First, since most families have just two children who are relatively close in age, older siblings are simply not available to take care of younger brothers or sisters. Second, smaller families have led to smaller networks of aunts and older cousins who formerly had been available for childcare. Compounding this, geographic mobility has decreased the likelihood that these few relatives live nearby. The possibility that grandparents or great aunts will live in the same house as parents with young children is becoming more and more rare. Over the past three decades there has been a steady decline in the number of families who "take in" older relatives and in the number of adults who live in a household. In the average household today there are only two adults; fewer than 4 percent of American children live in three-generational families. Finally, grandmothers and aunts increasingly have lives, homes, and jobs of their own and are therefore less likely to be available for babysitting.

CHANGING VALUES, NEW STRESS

The need for new kinds of childcare has also been fostered by changes in social values regarding the appropriate roles for parents and children. There has been a marked move away from the traditional notion that parents should devote their lives to their children, making sacrifices in their own comfort and personal lives to ensure that their children have it better than they did. In a recent survey of parents in 1,230 families with children under thirteen, all parents were less self-sacrificing than in the previous generation.[10] Forty-three percent of those interviewed reflected the attitudes of a "new breed" of parents, who reject conventional notions of marriage, religion, thrift, and toil. They are less child-oriented and more self-centered than their parents were and are raising their children to eat, play, dress, and do as they please. The goal for both parents and children in these families, it seems, is personal fulfillment. This new attitude frees parents from feeling that exclusive childcare is their *duty*.

Nonetheless, for young parents the net result of these social changes is likely to be psychological stress:

> Parents today are worried and uncertain about how to bring up their children. They feel unclear about the proper balance between permissiveness and firmness. They fear they are neglecting their children, yet they sometimes resent the demand their children make. [They] wonder whether they're doing a good job as parents, yet are unable to define just what a good job is. In droves they seek expert advice. And many prospective parents wonder whether they ought to have children at all . . . What is new . . . is the intensity of the malaise, the sense of having no guidelines or supports for raising children, the feelings of not being in control as parents, and the widespread sense of personal guilt for what seems to be going awry.[11]

In the survey identifying the new breed of parents, more than a third of the parents interviewed worried about the job they were doing of raising children. In Great Britain as well, the stresses of modern life are sufficient to drive a quarter of all the mothers of young children to doctors with symptoms of depression or anxiety.[12] Researchers have found that these symptoms and the concerns parents express are not related to particular events in their lives, such as death or an illness, but to the general stresses inherent in their life conditions, stresses that are greatest for poor mothers, for single mothers, and for working mothers.[13]

For a poor mother, these stresses include inadequate living conditions, or even concern about sheer survival for herself and her children. The single mother must endure the physical strain of doing everything herself, the social problem of isolation, the psychological prob-

lem of loneliness and bitterness, and the economic problem of reduced family income. The working married
mother has to cope not only with physical fatigue but
with conflict between her work and her husband's, concern about balancing her maternal, wifely, and employee
roles, and guilt about the harm she must be doing her
children. Even so-called new-breed parents think mothers of young children should work only if they have to
for economic reasons. More than two thirds of the parents in the survey thought children were worse off if their
mothers were working—including half of the mothers
who were working themselves.

All these kinds of stresses—fatigue, frustration, worry,
guilt, uncertainty—can lead to a mother's being de-
pressed or anxious and consequently less able to offer
adequate care and nurturance to her children. Once
again, to alleviate this stressful situation, there is a need
for daycare.

THE NEED FOR DAYCARE

It is clear from this catalogue of social changes that
many families are finding it desirable or necessary to
make arrangements for the daily care of their children
beyond what they themselves can provide. More and
more families are looking for more and more daycare. Is
it available?

In the United States, there are now nearly 8 million
preschool children whose mothers are working, and this
is expected to rise to 10.5 million in the next decade. Yet
there are at present fewer than 2 million places for children in daycare centers, fewer than in 1945. Most of the
remaining 6-plus million families make other arrangements—with aunts, babysitters, daycare homes, or nur-

sery schools—but there are still many thousands of children who are unsupervised or in the care of siblings under sixteen or relatives over sixty-five. Only 19 percent of those parents who want center care find openings for their children.[14] Such mothers will wait in line through the night before registration day for the few daycare places that are filled within hours.

Nor are things any better in Great Britain. While the number of women in the labor force has increased, there has been no increase in the number of daycare places. Provision of day nurseries is so meager that only five out of one hundred preschool children in single-parent families are looked after in government centers. In two surveys of parents of children under five in England and Wales, two thirds of the mothers wanted some kind of daycare (the majority, fulltime), but only one third were using it; the other third felt they could not find the daycare they needed of *any* kind.[15] In both countries, many more mothers would work or would return to work earlier if they could find daycare for their children; the most common reason for not working is that the daycare is not available.[16]

The evidence seems clear. In the United States, Great Britain, and Canada social forces have created a serious need for alternatives to the traditional childcare provided by a mother at home all day. The need is increasing rapidly as more and more mothers go to work without being able to rely on traditional family supports like babysitting big sisters and grandmothers. At the same time, in none of these countries has there been a concomitant increase in the number of daycare centers.

Why, then, in the face of such an obvious need, are daycare facilities so limited? Why haven't government or private groups stepped in to support the expansion of daycare services? Why isn't this a higher priority in public policy? The answer, I think, lies in the controversies evoked by daycare. These controversies go far beyond simply what is convenient for mothers. They strike at the core of our social system and our personal ideologies. They involve deep-seated psychological issues, social values, economic interests, and political ideals. These deep-seated beliefs lead people to strong positions on daycare, ranging from avid advocacy to adamant opposition. There is no simple agreement that would support the enlargement of daycare—or its elimination.

EXPERT OPINIONS

The diverse positions taken on daycare are clearly illustrated by the differing opinions of "experts" found in recent books, magazine articles, and television talk shows. On one side, child pyschoanalyst Selma Fraiberg paints the gloomiest possible picture—unstable babysitters, regimented daycare homes, daycare centers with fifteen children for every adult and a sorry collection of mangy toys. She strongly advises all mothers to stay home to provide their children with proper care and a stable human relationship.[17] Pediatrician Benjamin Spock agrees that in the first three years children need devoted, responsive, fulltime parental love and suggests that women who want to work should find careers they can follow at home.[18] And Burton White, author of the bestselling *The First Three Years of Life*, condones only parttime work for mothers, at best.[19] On the other side of the controversy, psychologist Bruno Bettelheim says that the notion that women's needs are fulfilled only through service to the family must change, and that daycare should be used by women who want to work as well as those who have to.[20] Developmentalist Jerome Kagan gives daycare a "clean bill of health."[21]

Clearly there is no consensus among the experts. What is more confusing, even the same expert may reverse his stand from one year to the next. Dr. Spock, for example, moved to a more favorable view of daycare between 1974 and 1976; Kagan's 1976 "clean bill of health" was a reversal of an earlier "daycare can be dangerous" stand in 1971; and psychoanalyst John Bowlby, whose earlier position ("maternal love in infancy is as important for mental health as vitamins and proteins for physical health") had been used to oppose daycare, expressed a more modulated view in 1980: "The last thing I want to see is a young mother cooped up all day every day with a baby or toddler and no assistance. I think the crucial thing is that the parents provide stable continuity, and on top of that one can build variety."[22]

There is a general trend toward a more positive view of daycare among child development experts, but still we find mixed reviews. Why do authorities, even those who are supposedly basing their opinions on scientific evidence, disagree? The answer lies in the tendency of experts (like everyone else) to read and interpret research and observations selectively, in order to support a view about daycare influenced by their own personal values.

PERSONAL VALUES

Although personal values come in an infinite variety of colors and stripes, for purposes of illustration they can be divided into two major camps: the "Righteous Right" and the "Liberated Left." Righteous Rightists hold values that give top priority to family, home, and mother. They admire the traditional myth of motherhood: mother's place is in the home, where her day can be spent guiding her children's paths with serene and sensitive wisdom through the pitfalls of bad companions, junk food, and TV violence, toward the American dream of success and fulfillment, and where she can be available to greet her tired husband at day's end with a smile, soothing candle-light, and gourmet cuisine, after the charming children have been presented and put to bed. They ascribe to an ideal of family as alone and self-sufficient, creating inde-pendent and unique individuals who make it on their own in a competitive society. Righteous Rightists oppose daycare because it clashes with their family ideal and myths of motherhood; it removes mother from the house and sullies her virtue in the marketplace. It removes chil-dren from home and mother. It impedes the development of children's individualism by group rearing. It encour-ages families to rely on others (the state or private enter-prise) for assistance in childcare rather than maintaining their own vital self-sufficiency.

Liberated Leftists place at the top of their priorities the rights of women and the poor. They maintain that citi-zens and governments have a responsibility to uphold these rights for all. The myth of motherhood they have created is the feminist ideal of mother as interesting, happy, and satisfied because she can attain fulfillment in a career or meaningful work. They support daycare be-cause they see it as a way of liberating women from the bonds of childrearing and because it will offer mothers a choice of roles so that they can realize their equal rights. Daycare increases the self-sufficiency of families by en-abling them to earn larger incomes. And it promotes indi-vidual achievement by providing educational services for children who otherwise would not have such intellectual stimulation.

"Liberated Left" and "Righteous Right" are stereotypes

of the two extremes in personal values that influence the views of experts and parents regarding daycare. But while most people fall in between these extremes, the distribution of such widely opposing values in the population has made it impossible to reach agreement in our society about supporting or expanding daycare.

POLITICAL AND PRACTICAL ISSUES

There are other obstacles to enlarging daycare besides divergent personal values. One is simply the problem of finding financial support for any social services in governments when their economies are plagued by the inflation, unemployment, skyrocketing costs, and decreasing productivity found today in most Western nations. Although the need for daycare services is enormous, so are the costs. As a service, daycare is expensive to provide, and it is hard to reduce costs without reducing quality. Many service-oriented organizations, including governments, unions, churches, and charitable agencies, have therefore been reluctant to make a large investment. As a business venture, running a daycare center is not very profitable, and few commercial organizations or independent entrepreneurs have been attracted to this market.

Then there is a political problem: daycare is not represented by a strong, vocal, and unified lobby or interest group. One important obstacle is the unresolved issue of who would staff daycare facilities. There is a clear need for more trained personnel, but who should they be? Schoolteachers, early-childhood educators, social workers, nursery nurses, child development aides, or cooperating parents are possibilities. Though ultimately there could be room for all of them, at present there are more competitive than cooperative efforts among them. With the decline in the number of school-age children and the desire to bolster their own positions, teachers and their unions point to the benefits of existing administrative systems and available trained personnel in the public school system. Just as adamantly, opponents of this perceived takeover by the educational establishment point to the disadvantages of a system mired in bureaucracy and overpaid teachers who are trained to work with older children. Resolving such arguments is necessary before those persons concerned about expanding daycare can form a unified political force.

Another impediment lies in the problem of how daycare should be regulated and what the regulatory standards should be. In the United States, a long, drawn-out battle over standards has involved hundreds of daycare providers, parents, child development experts, and legislators, and dozens of hearings, laws, and revisions since the early 1970s. The issues they have argued about include cost, quality, space and size, nutrition, health care, staff training, adult-child ratios, monitoring, and reporting; and each group has its own views, not always compatible with the rest. Now, even though some guidelines for minimal daycare standards have finally been agreed upon (described in Chapter 9), there has been no move toward implementing them. Until all these interest groups resolve their differences and push forcefully for acceptable standards, it is unlikely that public support for daycare or daycare regulation will be forthcoming.

FEARS ABOUT THE CHILDREN

An important deterrent to daycare expansion has been the fears of many that it will have harmful effects on children. One source of these fears is the pathetic picture painted by early studies of children raised in residential institutions such as orphanages and asylums.[23] In the eighteenth century a staggering death rate of children in these institutions was recorded: in Dublin, for example, of 10,000 children admitted to a foundling home, only 45 survived. A hundred years later, with advances in hygiene and medical care, the mortality rate for these children was vastly improved, but physicians noticed that children in orphanages were scrawny, apathetic, and severely retarded. These flaws were attributed to "bad blood," and nothing was done to change things. Not until the 1940s was it first recognized that something about the environment in these orphanages might be responsible for the dire outcomes observed. The something that was fixed on was the lack of a mother's love. It is this old view that has sometimes been used in arguments against daycare, by suggesting that children of working mothers, who are in fulltime daycare, will similarly be deprived of maternal love.

But children in daycare are not deprived of mother love or even maternal care; they have that love and care before they are placed in daycare and continue to experience it at the end of every day. Mothers don't put their children in daycare because they don't love them. What is more, the retarded children in the old orphanages were deprived of much more than maternal love. They had little affection or attention from anyone. Attendants were few and always changing; they could not give individual children continuous, consistent, warm, or responsive care. The children were also in poor physical surroundings, with minimal health care, inadequate food, nothing interesting to look at or play with. There were no programs of education or exercise. These conditions are not found in most daycare centers today. Studies of residential care, whether old or new, simply cannot be used to suggest that daycare is harmful to children's development.

Still, fears about harmful effects of daycare have persisted. One particular concern focuses on the relationship between child and mother. Psychologists have demonstrated that it is essential to healthy emotional development for an infant to have a close and continuing relationship with one caring adult over the first several years of life. The question is, Does that adult have to be the mother? Or if it is the mother, does she have to be the exclusive caregiver? How many adult caregivers can be involved before it becomes too much for the child? What will it mean if children are raised by strangers or professionals rather than by family? After a close relationship with the mother or professional is established, is it harmful for the child to be separated from that adult? What will happen if children are cared for by a changing cast of caregivers who will inevitably have different childrearing styles and values? In the absense of solid answers to these questions, many parents and professionals have feared the worst.

They also wonder what effect daycare will have on children's intellectual development. Researchers have demonstrated that stimulation in the form of adult attention, conversation, and play is critical for children's intellectual development in the preschool years. In a daycare facility with a group of children and few caregivers, can sufficient adult attention be given each child to ensure his or her intellectual growth? And what about the child's social development? We have all observed that even very young children behave quite differently when they are with other children from how they act with their parents. Will children who are raised in groups be more dependent on their peers? Or will they be more aggressive toward other children? Or more withdrawn and passive? Will they conform to normal adult standards for socially acceptable behavior, such as courtesy, cooperation, reasonable competition? Will they learn to control their impulses? Will they retain their individuality? Once again, in the absence of data to answer these questions, many have feared the worst. These fears, too, will have to be allayed before daycare can be solidly supported.

All these problems and controversies—divergent personal values, varied expert opinions, practical and political obstacles, fears about the effects of daycare on children's development—have held back daycare expansion. The problems are profound and complex, unlikely to be resolved easily or in the near future. Two basic kinds of change are likely needed before daycare can expand in any meaningful way. One would involve the dissemination of research results showing that group care does not have the harmful effects some have feared. The other would be the occurrence of broader social and economic factors overturning current practical obstacles to daycare provision. For in the past there have been some booms in daycare, and major, if temporary, expansion has occurred. Perhaps it will again, despite current difficulties. In the next chapter we look back over the past century and a half to see how daycare services have waxed and waned in conjunction with other social changes.

3 / History

Daycare is not a new phenomenon. Its history as a formal, recognized service goes back well into the last century. Its popularity has increased and decreased with changes in social, economic, and political circumstances. And it is useful for us to consider the history of daycare and these changes so we can better understand how the current situation has evolved and what the future is likely to hold.

THE UNITED STATES

To trace the history of daycare in America, we must follow two streams: those of the day nursery and the nursery school.[1]

The first day nursery   The first day nurseries were a response to the flood of immigration that brought more than 5 million foreign families to the United States between 1815 and 1860, and to the industrialization and urbanization that took women from their homes to factories during this period. Young children were left to fend for themselves—locked up at home, allowed to roam the streets, or put under the casual supervision of a neighbor or sibling. The situation was ripe for philanthropic intervention, and wealthy women and well-meaning service organizations, appalled by the neglect, vice, and lack of sanitation, organized day nurseries to provide care for these children. The first American day nursery was opened in Boston in 1838 by Mrs. Joseph Hale to provide care for the children of seamen's working wives and widows. Sixteen years later, the Nurses and Children's Hospital in New York City opened its version of the day nursery to care for infants and toddlers of working women who had been patients there. A day nursery opened in Philadelphia in 1863 to care for children of working women in hospitals and factories during the Civil War. And in 1893 a model day nursery set up by the World Fair in Chicago cared for 10,000 children of visitors. By 1898, about 175 day nurseries were operating in various parts of the country, enough to warrant the creation of a National Federation of Day Nurseries.

Over the next decade, expansion of daycare continued. Day nurseries were most often set up in converted homes. They were open six days a week, twelve hours a day. Most of them were simply "custodial," run by overworked matrons with one or two assistants, who had to do the laundry, cooking, and cleaning as well as look after the children. Day nurseries did not have the benefit of public support, monetary or ideological; the day nursery was considered a last resort for children who couldn't be cared for at home.

A few day nurseries with more energetic directors offered not only clean, safe places to keep children but something of interest to occupy their time. Since the clientele were largely immigrants, these centers taught children manners and hygiene in the American mode. Children were trained to use a napkin, to eat in silence, to march in line, and were given tickets (comparable to tokens or gold stars in some modern preschool programs) redeemable for articles of clothing for exhibiting the American virtues of punctuality, obedience, industry, cleanliness, and good behavior. Beginning in the 1890s, some of the better day nurseries also began to offer a modest educational program, by hiring kindergarten teachers to come in and teach the children for several hours a day. The "curriculum" was extended in these exceptional day nurseries to include weaving, sewing, reading, spelling, and paper folding.

Underlying the establishing of these day nurseries was the notion that these mothers needed help, and clients were selected on that basis. Consequently, in the better day nurseries, working mothers were also offered services beyond a place to leave their children. They were offered classes in sewing, cooking, English, and childcare, access to job training and opportunities, and help with practical family problems. In the 1920s they were also given help with family-centered psychological problems.

The 1930s and 1940s. In 1933, to alleviate effects of the Great Depression, President Roosevelt initiated the Federal Economic Recovery Act and the Work Projects Administration. Public funds for the expansion of daycare became available for the first time. The reason was to supply jobs for unemployed teachers, nurses, cooks, and janitors. By 1937 these programs had set up 1,900 day nurseries, caring for 40,000 children. These nurseries were most commonly located in schools and followed school hours; there was increased participation by teachers and an increased emphasis on the older—educable—preschool child.

This daycare "boomlet" was short-lived. With the demise of the WPA in 1938, day nurseries declined until

World War II. Then, with the massive mobilization of women into war-related industries and renewed financial support provided by the Lanham Act (1942), the prejudice against working women (superseded apparently by patriotism) disappeared, and day nurseries flourished. By 1945, more than a million and a half children were in daycare. This time, the programs were more innovative. In Los Angeles, for example, the Gale Manor Apartments turned its ground floor into a combination nursery and playground and accepted as tenants only working parents with children. In Portland, Oregon, the Kaiser Shipbuilding Corporation opened two daycare centers, one at the entrance to each of its shipyards, and these centers provided not only supervision for the children of women working in the shipyards but the staffs did shopping and mending, made doctors' appointments for the mothers, cared for children with minor illnesses, and offered carryout dinners at low cost to mothers who worked long hours.

From 1950 to 1965. This boom in daycare facilities ended as precipitously as it had begun, with the end of the war and the withdrawal of Lanham funds in 1946. Nearly 3,000 centers closed, and by 1950 only 18,000 children were in daycare centers. From 1950 to 1965, daycare again became a marginal service for the poor with an emphasis on social work and problem families. Unexpectedly, however, although the centers closed, women did not return as anticipated to their "rightful" place in the home. They continued to work, and those who were not poor enough to qualify for publicly supported daycare used the few available private daycare centers or made other arrangements with relatives, neighbors, or housekeepers.

Only in the mid 1960s did attitudes toward daycare begin to become more positive as it was recognized that mothers were already working and as it seemed that provision of daycare would allow more women to get off the welfare rolls. Federal support for daycare became available once more, though still only for poor families. This change in attitude and legislation was influenced also by what was happening in early childhood education, for in the mid-1960s the two streams, day nurseries and nursery schools, began to converge.

Nursery schools. While day nurseries were supposed primarily to solve the problems of the poor, nursery schools were intended to provide enrichment for the affluent. The first cooperative nursery school was started by faculty wives at the University of Chicago in 1915. Its purpose was to offer their youngsters an opportunity for wholesome play, to give the mothers some hours of leisure away from the children, and to try a social venture of cooperation. The idea caught on quickly, and many more schools began in the following two decades. Most of these early nursery schools were all-day programs (8:30 to 4:30), located in converted residences, and supported by parent fees and participation. Children as young as eighteen months were fed, toileted, amused, and given social training. Parent education was often part of the program and parent participation was required, but nursery schools were above all for children. They offered a rich physical environment with blocks, sand, clay, and paints where children could play freely on their own without their mothers' supervision under the kindly guidance of an educated but unintrusive teacher, whose purpose was to help the children develop impulse control, verbal skills, and knowledge about the world. Nursery schools were popular with middle-class families from the 1930s to 1960s.

The convergence. In the 1960s a new focus on the preschool period added energy to nursery school education and led to a merging of this stream with the daycare stream. As an outgrowth of the furor surrounding the launching of Sputnik and Americans' desire to catch up, people focused their attention on early childhood as a critical period for stimulating intellectual development. They hoped for later benefits in scientific progress and national achievement. From 1967 to 1970, enrollment in nursery schools and voluntary kindergartens increased markedly (from a quarter to a half of all eligible three-to-five-year-olds), and enrollment in licensed daycare centers doubled. At the same time, these programs shifted to a more developmental, academic emphasis, and a number of experimental programs designed specifically to foster children's intellectual growth were set up. Most significantly, in 1965 a new national program that provided nursery-school education for poor children was instituted, Project Head Start. This program was the first major government involvement in early childhood programs, except in times of national emergency. It was only a part-day program and did not really serve the needs of working mothers, but it was significant because it focused public attention on the idea that education was important for all young children, not just those in affluent families. It also opened the possibility of government support for educational daycare. At the same time, in this climate of anticipation of the benefits of early childhood education, child development professionals, middle-class parents, and women's groups were pressing for educational or "developmental" daycare. Public funds for daycare were made available through a variety of federal programs in the late 1960s.

The ball was rolling, and efforts and optimism reached a peak in the early 1970s: the 1970 White House Conference on Children selected daycare as the most serious problem confronting American families and children, and the Comprehensive Child Development Act of 1971, recommending comprehensive and educational daycare not only for poor and handicapped children but for all children on a sliding fee scale, passed the Senate and the House of Representatives. The dream that Act represented was shattered by President Nixon's veto in December 1971.

Since that time, fifteen to twenty daycare-related bills have been presented to Congress every session. Only a handful have passed, and in no way do they provide comprehensive daycare. The official policy in the United States today is more implicit than explicit: federal subsidies for childcare for the poor through Social Security and tax credits for childcare for everyone else. Despite the lack of government initiative, however, there has been a greater than 30 percent increase in daycare-center enrollment since 1970 (greater than 70 percent for children under two). Much of this is due to an increase in commercial daycare. Kinder-Care, a commercial daycare chain, for example, increased from 60 centers in 1974 to 280 in 1978 to 340 in 1979.

GREAT BRITAIN

The current daycare situation in Great Britain is not unlike that in the United States; and though their paths were separate, there are historical parallels in daycare developments in the two countries.[2] One similarity is in the separate childcare streams for rich and poor: nursery schools and day nurseries.

Day nurseries. One of the most appalling aspects of the life of the poor in nineteenth-century Great Britain was the death rate for children under five. Some 70 of every thousand poor children did not survive—the terrible result of crowding, starvation, and disease in the cities, of neglect, drugs, malnutrition, and lack of physical or health care in rural areas. Infant mortality was especially high in families where the mother worked. Mothers were given no maternity leave, and their children were left unattended or given out to a neighbor for care. Such care, uncontrolled and uninspected, was almost always unsatisfactory. An alternative used by a small number was the "dame school," in which many small children were crowded into a dirty, ill-ventilated tenement or cellar. If the elderly or invalid woman in charge had any education, she might try to give the children some instruction in the alphabet and reading.

Day nurseries were a response to this situation. The first English day nursery opened in London in 1850, with admission contingent on the recommendation of a clergyman or other respectable person. But fees were high, and the experiment with this and a few similar day nurseries was not successful. More promising were the free day nurseries, which opened first in Manchester in 1871. By 1906 there were 30 day nurseries, and a National Society of Day Nurseries was formed. These nurseries provided adequate physical care for preschool children, but their numbers were tiny compared with the need. Not until World War I, when women were needed in munition factories, was there a major expansion of daycare facilities. At this time, public funding for nurseries became available through the Maternity and Child Welfare Act of 1918, and by the next year, 174 day nurseries had been started. After the war, the number of day nurseries again dropped drastically, not to increase again until World War II.

Beginning in 1940, day nurseries and nursery centers where children could play and learn social skills were set up by the Ministry of Health in areas where there were war evacuees or a shortage of female workers. They were open twelve to fifteen hours a day and available to working mothers for their preschool children on payment of a fee. The number of daycare facilities in England and Wales expanded rapidly from 194 fulltime centers in 1941 to 1,450 in 1944.

As before, however, these faded away after the war. The Ministry discouraged mothers of young children from working and suggested that mothers of older children send them to nursery schools. Daycare services were to be used only by families with special needs. From 1945 to the late 1960s, government-subsidized day nurseries declined in numbers from 1,600 to 466. As in the United States, working mothers had to make private arrangements for alternative childcare, and an increase was observed in the number of registered childminders and private nurseries.

Nursery schools. A separate path was being followed all this time in nursery education, a path reflecting the familiar dichotomy between day nurseries as a necessary evil and nursery schools as a positive opportunity.

The first British nursery school was started by industrialist-reformer Robert Owen at the New Lanark cotton mill in Scotland in 1816. It offered supervised care for children of women working in the mill, but its emphasis was educational. Children were admitted from the time they could walk and say a few words, and stayed until they were of school age. This first nursery school was a model of kindliness, good sense, and child-centered cheerfulness. Its curriculum consisted of singing, dancing, marching, fife-playing, geography, and outdoor free play. No books or formal instruction was permitted.

This school was the exception rather than the rule, however, in its accommodation to the explicit concerns of working mothers and in its nondidactic approach to education. Because Owen was an atheist, he was not as influential in Great Britain as an opposing figure, Samuel Wilderspin, a sanctimonious pedagogue who toured the nation from 1824 to 1834, promoting his brand of nursery education. Following his advice, all over the country educators set up infant schools. These schools consisted of tiered galleries in which classes of sixty to one hundred young children sat in rows on benches with the teacher standing in front, teaching the 3 R's by rote. This dreary environment was typical of nursery education until the beginning of the 1900s, when the Board of Education condemned early schooling because it dulled children's imaginations and weakened their powers of observation. As a consequence, in more progressive schools benches were replaced by movable desks and some toys were provided. But formal drilling in the 3 R's continued, and, as late as 1926, the Code of Regulation for Public Elementary Schools in England stipulated that recreation periods for classes of children under five must not exceed thirty minutes.

In 1933, a report by the Consultative Committee on Infant and Nursery Schools recommended that nursery schools emphasize children's physical well-being and intellectual development through a teacher-guided "unfolding" of children's natural powers. This started a shift toward more open and informal nursery education. Over the next five years, the number of such open nursery schools increased to 118. World War II with its expansion of day nurseries intervened, but nursery schools continued to increase after the war (when day nurseries declined) to 353 in 1947. The nursery schools offered half-day programs of informal educational activities, which may have been fine for children but did not serve the needs of fulltime working mothers.

Nannies and playgroups   In Great Britain there was also a third path of childcare for the upper classes. From 1800 to World War II, affluent families employed nannies to care for their children. At the beginning of this century there were as many as half a million nannies in England. Only during World War II, when young women found they could get better-paying jobs outside domestic service, were these mothers faced with the same problems working-class mothers had faced for a century and a half. This led many middle-class mothers to interest themselves in the playgroup movement. Playgroups for preschool children had begun in New Zealand and spread to England and Europe. Groups of mothers met regularly in one another's homes to share activities with their children. By 1965, there were 500 such groups in England; in 1972, there were more than 15,000. But although playgroups offered social enrichment for mothers and their children, they were only part-time, too, and didn't help working mothers.

1960s to the present.   The 1960s in Great Britain, as in the United States, saw some convergence of the streams of childcare in a series of government reports and acts.

The Plowden Report in 1967 concluded that part-time nursery education for children over two was good for children and parents; the Seebohm Report in 1968 recommended that additional nursery places be made in day nurseries, in playgroups, and with childminders for children from large families or with isolated, sick, or single mothers; and the Urban Aid Program allowed money to be paid from the Treasury in urban areas of special need for nursery schools, nursery classes, day nurseries, and playgroups. Still, there was no major expansion of these programs, and no particular concern for working mothers. A White Paper in 1972 recommended providing nursery school places for 90 percent of all four-year-olds by 1981. But this was the overly optimistic highpoint of early education enthusiasm. Shortly after, the British economy lurched out of control, and education and welfare systems had to fight for mere survival, not expansion. As in the United States, the possibility of enlarging facilities for daycare or nursery education through public support had been shelved. The situation is likely to continue unless major social, economic, political, or informational changes once more intervene.

4 / Here and Now

We have seen that the current need for alternative child-care far exceeds the supply of licensed facilities. What arrangements have parents had to make as a result of this shortage?

Table 2 shows the distribution of the major types of care arrangements currently being used in the United States and Great Britain. In both countries the majority of children are taken care of by relatives (55 percent in the United States; 67 percent in the United Kingdom). Most often, this occurs in the child's own home. The next most common arrangement for the care of children of working mothers is care by a woman who is not related to the child (32 percent in the United States; 22 percent in the United Kingdom). This occurs most frequently in the home of the caregiver. Finally, the least common arrangement is the formal daycare center (13 percent in the United States; 11 percent in the United Kingdom).

CARE IN THE CHILD'S HOME

Care in the home while a mother is at work may be provided by the father, grandmother, older sibling, neighbor, friend, babysitter, nanny, housekeeper, maid, live-in student, or *au pair*. This may be the most common form of "daycare," but it is the one about which we know

Table 2. Childcare Arrangements for Preschool Children
of Working Mothers

	% Children using arrangement	
Care arrangement	U.S.	U.K.
In own home		
Father	20	37
Other relative	20	20
Nonrelated babysitter	12	11
Daycare home		
Relative	15	10
Nonrelative	20	11
Daycare center	13	11
	100	100

These figures are for children under six years old in the U.S. and five years old in the U.K. They do not include children whose mothers take them to work or work at home, or occasional care such as a playgroup. Statistics are approximate based on most recent available data from the U.S. Department of Labor and the U.K. Office of Population Censuses and Surveys.

least. It simply has not been studied—perhaps because it is so private, because it varies so much from home to home, or because it seems to be so much like care by the mother.

It is obvious that, compared to other more formal kinds of daycare, this in-home care offers many advantages. The hours are flexible, there is no need for the child or parent to travel, the child remains in a familiar, secure place, and the mother is able, to some extent, to monitor the behavior of a caregiver who becomes increasingly better known to her. In-home care keeps siblings together, and the caregiver can provide each child with personalized attention. This care arrangement may be relatively economical if there are several children in the family, if care is provided as a favor to the parents, in exchange, or out of a sense of family duty, or if other services like shopping or laundry are included. If the in-home caregiver is related to the child, this turns out to be the most stable of all daycare arrangements.[1]

On the other hand, the arrangement has disadvantages. The caregiver is usually untrained and unlicensed, and may or may not provide good care. (If she is trained, it becomes the most expensive kind of daycare.) If no relative is available, it may be hard to find an in-home caregiver because a systematic referral system does not exist. And since, when the caregiver is not related, this form of care is the most unstable, frequently having to replace caregivers may be a frustrating drawback. There is also a relative disadvantage for the child in in-home care since educational or group activities with peers are less likely to occur. Beyond these obvious advantages and disadvantages, daycare in the child's home is an unknown commodity of infinite variety; we have no solid assessment of its quality.

DAYCARE HOMES AND CHILDMINDERS

A second form of daycare that is popular in the United States and Canada is the daycare home. It may be licensed or unlicensed; the caregiver (daycare home provider) may be related or unrelated, trained or untrained; the number of children may range from one to six (family daycare home) or six to twelve (group daycare home). The basis for this arrangement ranges from an informal agreement about shared caregiving between friends to a highly formal, supervised network of licensed homes.

Daycare homes have a number of distinct advantages as a form of care. They are usually nearby and children can walk there; they are in a familiar neighborhood where people are likely to share the parents' values and circumstances. The mother has more control over what happens to her child than she would in a daycare center; she can give instructions to a daycare home provider that she would not be able to give a daycare center teacher. A caregiver is usually flexible about taking children of different ages and in adjusting her hours to the mother's schedule. She may accept children with special needs or handicaps who wouldn't be accepted in a center. For a family with one or two children, a daycare home is a relatively economical form of care. For the child, this kind of care offers the advantages of new experiences he wouldn't have at home, relations with a different family, usually with other children of different ages, and often with a man in the house; yet it provides continuity with the kind of family care he is used to, in a home, with real-life activities, with a "mother figure," and only a small group of children. A daycare provider, like an in-home caregiver, can devote individual attention to the children in her charge. If the provider is part of a training and support network, a daycare home also has the advantages of accessibility, stability, and adherence to health and safety standards; the caregiver has some training in childcare; and regular consultation with child development professionals is possible.

This kind of daycare has disadvantages as well. A major one is that of the different types of caregivers a daycare home provider is the least accountable to parents for her actions. A daycare home is not open for public inspection, and after the mother drops off her child, though she may instruct the caregiver, she has no knowledge of what really happens. Babies may be screamers but they are not squealers. The vast majority of daycare home providers are not trained, not part of a support network, and not licensed. They are unlikely to offer formal instruction or organized educational activities, and the physical equipment they have is not as plentiful or as varied as in most daycare centers.

Researchers have now begun to study this kind of daycare. One of the first studies was a survey of homes and centers throughout the United States carried out by the National Council of Jewish Women under the direction of Mary Keyserling.[2] Their report, published in 1972 and aptly called *Windows on Day Care* rated daycare homes from poor to superior. Fourteen percent of the daycare homes they visted were rated poor. For example, they found "seven or eight children, one year or under, most strapped to kitchen chairs, all seemingly in a stupor." Forty-eight percent were rated fair, 31 percent good, and only 7 percent superior. A number of studies since the Keyserling survey have made more systematic and detailed observations.[3] The largest and most recent of these is the National Day Care Home Study, which included 350 daycare homes in twenty-five cities, with more detailed interviews and observations made in Los Angeles, San Antonio, and Philadelphia. Putting together the findings from all these studies, we get a picture of life in a typical daycare home.

Nearly all daycare homes provide all-day care and give the children lunch and snacks. They usually are single-family homes with outdoor play areas. Most have only one to three children present at one time. These children tend to be in the 18- to 36-month range. In nearly half, the children include one of the daycare home provider's own. The typical provider is married, in her thirties, a high-school graduate with six years of daycare experience. Her husband is stably employed and makes a comfortable income. She is providing daycare because she is fond of children as well as for the money. She provides a positive, supportive environment: in the National Day Care Home Study, 94 percent of the home providers were observed to smile and laugh while only 31 percent of them were observed to scowl or act angry. All providers controlled the children by directives and suggestions rather than by physical punishment. On the average, they spent about half of their time involved with the children and the rest of the time on housework or personal activities. When they interacted with the children, in addition to feeding, washing, and dressing them, they chatted, labeled objects, explained and demonstrated how things work, read stories, and played games. They did not give formal lessons. The children spent about half of their time playing alone with sand, water, clay, and toys. Usually they were actively involved in their play, not crying, fighting, or aimlessly wandering about. They interacted with the caregiver only 13 percent of the time they were in her home and with peers only 5 percent. Although television was watched in most daycare homes, children spent only 7 percent of their time in that activity.

Of course these are just averages. There really is no typical daycare home. There is an infinite variety in homes and providers, just as there is in mothers. In age, the providers in the National Day Care Home Study ranged from twenty to sixty-nine; their education ranged from junior high to college graduation; they had from one month to thirty-six years of experience. There was also great variation in the kind of care they gave the children. This was related to whether they were licensed or part of a training network and to how much they viewed themselves as professional caregivers. Daycare home providers who were licensed or, even better, part of a network and who considered themselves professionals, who read childcare books, went to meetings, took classes in child development, and kept records on the children, were more likely to talk, help, teach, and play with the children and to provide a better physical environment with more music, dancing, books, educational TV, and nutritious food. Those who were doing it only because no better job was available, or as an informal agreement with friends, neighbors, or relatives, were less interactive and stimulating and spent more time on housework.

Daycare homes are also a common form of childcare in Great Britain. All daycare home providers, called childminders, who are paid and who care for children more than two hours a day at least one day a week are required to register with the Social Services Department. This is not enforced, though, and it is not known how many unregistered childminders there are. As in the United States, there are horror stories of "seven small children in one room ranged along a table being fed from the same bowl with the same spoon" or "a child tied by a clothesline to the kitchen table so as to stop him knocking over the paraffin heater whilst the minder went shopping,"[4] but no one knows how common such situations are.

There have been several recent attempts to make some observations of life at the childminder's.[5] Like the American daycare home provider, the typical English childminder is in her thirties, married with children of her own, and lives in a comfortable home with a garden. She too went into childcare because she was fond of children. The childminder sees her role as providing for children's physical needs, not as offering them education, play, and enrichment or as being sensitive to their emotional feelings and problems. When researchers in one study asked childminders what sort of person makes a good minder, the most common kind of response they got was:

> Someone with lots of patience and time. You've got to be able to cope with all sorts of children.
> I think you must never promise them anything you can't fulfill, and be fair to them and tolerant.
> Someone who doesn't mind having kids running around. It's no good if you want the house to look just so.

The responses suggested

> a view of minding as warm-hearted, accepting, relatively passive caretaking. Very few mentioned any outgoing qualities. Less than a fifth, for example, suggested a minder should should be prepared to play with or "talk to children on their own level," and only four minders suggested that she should be imaginative or have ideas for doing things with children. Turning towards the sorts of things they thought a minder should know about, [they] found that top of the list came first aid, which was put forward by half the minders. Second came commonsense or experience, or the knowledge you get from bringing up your own, which were suggested by one third, followed by knowing things "about children's play," suggested by 29 percent. Knowing about children's feelings or about problems (such as illnesses or special needs) appeared very low down in the list.[6]

Children at the minder's were incorporated into the minder's family, not given special attention. Only 30 percent of the childminders in this study reported that they had carried out specific educational or entertaining activities with the children, such as painting, reading, cutting out, playing with plasticine, blocks, or tiddlywinks, on the previous day. Instead, the children watched TV and the minder, played in the garden, went to the shops, and had tea. A brief vignette gives an idea of a typical day at the minder's home:

> Terry (age 2) arrived at 9 a.m. and started playing with the minder's own son of two. For the first part of the morning both the boys went around with the minder wherever she went, into the kitchen to tidy up and upstairs to make the beds. Then they watched "Playschool" with the minder in the same room. They all stayed in the livingroom, the children playing around the minder. A friend and her two children came for lunch. After lunch they all stayed in the livingroom while the minder fed her eleven-month-old baby. Then the children all went into the garden while the adults did the washing-up and chatted. The children were in and out, and eventually everyone went into the garden. Then the friend left, and Terry and the minder's son watched the children's television with the minder in the same room. Terry was collected at 5 p.m.[7]

Life at the childminder's is more like life at home than life at school, but it offers children less interaction with an adult than they would probably have with their mother at home.

In England networks to train, supervise, and support childminders are just beginning. There has been no opportunity to see if this will improve the quality of care provided. Unlike American daycare home providers, there do not seem to be any professional childminders and so far studies have not found that training or more experience makes childminders any more actively involved with the children.

DAYCARE CENTERS

A daycare center is the most visible and easily identi-fied alternative childcare arrangement, the one most peo-ple are referring to when they speak of daycare. A center (or day nursery) may provide care for fewer that fifteen children or more than three hundred; on the average there are fifty (American) or thirty (British) children in a center. They are usually divided into classes according to their age. The average class size is ten for infants and tod-dlers, seventeen for three-year-olds, nineteen for four-year-olds, and twenty for five-year-olds. Most children in daycare centers are three or four years old. Teachers in the centers tend to be young and of the same race as the children.

Compared to other daycare arrangements, centers have certain advantages. For the most part, they are relatively stable, keep predictable hours, and are publicly account-able and easily monitored by parents. They usually have some staff with training in child development and are likely to offer children educational opportunities and the chance to play with other children in a child-oriented, child-sized, safe environment that is rich in materials and equipment. They may offer health services as well. On the other hand, daycare centers are often located at some distance from the child's home, have less flexible hours, do not offer care for sick children, are more expensive, and are less available because of strict eligibility criteria.

Like daycare homes, centers run the gamut from poor to excellent. In the American study by Keyserling men-tioned before, 30 percent of the centers visited were rated as poor. For example, "over 20 children huddled in too small, poorly ventilated, cement floor area" or "babies kept in 'cages'—double-decker cardboard cribs in one room with open gas heaters." Forty-three percent were rated fair, 21 percent good, and only 5 percent superior. These ratings were even lower than the ratings of day-care homes made in the study. But it is not fair to jump to the conclusion that center care is worse than home care. A range of quality is found in both kinds of setting.

More recent and extensive studies have attempted to detail the differences in "ecology" of these two forms of daycare.[8] They show that, on the average, physical conditions (space, ventilation, light, toilets, cleanliness, toys, safety, nutrition, and immunization) are better in daycare centers, while daycare homes rank higher in social-personal conditions (more adults per child, more interaction with the caregiver, more conversation, more socialization attempts, more emotional input, and more sensitive approaches to the child by the caregiver). Learning occurs in both settings, but it is likely to be of different kinds: in the daycare homes observed there was more free exploration, "messing around," casual learning in real-life tasks with real role models. A question from the caregiver, "What would you like for lunch?" could lead to a long discussion about finding something everyone likes, which foods are more nutritious, what ingredients are necessary, how long it takes to prepare, and so on. In centers there was more interaction among children, more formal educational activities, more questions from the caregiver, and more rules to follow. A comment about food might lead to a "mini lesson" consisting of questions posed by the teacher like "Are peas a vegetable?", "How many vegetables can you name?", and "What colors are they?"

Although there is immense variation among daycare centers, some differences can be predicted by knowing the type of center: franchised or independent, cooperative or commercial, and so on. A major difference between centers relates to the source of support: private (supported by parent fees) or public (supported by government funds). Differences between these two major types of center are summarized in Table 3.[9] Remembering that these are only averages, it is clear that for all counts on which there is a difference, and there is a difference on most, public daycare centers come out ahead. Public centers are more likely to have a trained staff, to offer a comprehensive program with a child development component, and to adhere to a higher set of standards. Let us look at some of the variations within the public and private types of daycare center.

Proprietary centers. These are private daycare centers run for profit. About half the centers in the United States are of this type; they are less common in Britain. Proprietary centers have no eligibility criteria and will take anyone who can pay the fee (which is likely to be lower than other daycare centers). Usually they are quite small, enrolling about thirty children, and often located in converted stores or shops. They are typically "Ma and Pa" family-run operations, staffed by the owner and one or two assistants who are not professionally trained. Their clientele tend to be homogeneous and from the neighborhood in which they are located. They have less recreational space and equipment and fewer educational activities than other daycare centers. They offer no social or health services. Parents do not usually participate in the program, simply dropping their children off in the morning and picking them up at night.

Commercial centers. These are also private, profit-making centers. They account for only about 6 percent of the

Table 3. Differences between Private and Public
Daycare Centers

Category	Private	Public
Children		
Size of class	17	19
Staff		
Number	4	8
Adult-child ratio	1:8	1:6
Teacher education	14 yrs.	14 yrs.
Teachers trained in child development	44%	66%
Teachers' experience in daycare	5 yrs.	4 yrs.
Teachers' time in present center	2 yrs.	3 yrs.
Parents		
Participation as volunteers	12%	45%
Decisions on policy	12%	61%
Cost (in 1978)	$1300	$2500
Ratings		
Superior	1%	10%
Good	15%	28%
Fair	35%	51%
Poor	50%	11%
Other services	—	Screening, testing, immunization, transportation, social work, referral to other agencies or professionals

available daycare centers now, but in the United States, at least, they are on the increase. There has been a dramatic rise in so-called "Kentucky Fried" daycare chains since 1970. Kinder-Care, Mary Moppet, and Children's World are examples of successful commercial ventures. All the centers in a chain have uniform facilities and programs. Developing a model and then replicating or franchising it on a large scale has apparently made daycare a reasonable business undertaking. So has paying staff the minimum wage. On the average, these centers enroll seventy to one hundred children in classes of about twenty. They are well equipped, in new buildings, with nutritional food and some educational activities. They tend to emphasize the quality of the physical facility over the quality of the staff.

Community church centers. Thirty-five percent of the daycare centers in the United States are run by private community or charitable organizations, churches, companies, or cooperating parents. Those run by community or church organizations are usually for children from poor families. They emphasize personal attention and affection from caregivers (who may be volunteers) rather than physical facilities. They are often located in old buildings, such as the church or community hall, and have limited recreational facilities. They do not stress health care, social services, or education.

Company centers. In small numbers, corporations, factories, hospitals, universities, and trade unions have provided daycare as a fringe benefit for their employees. Usually the center is at a site near the company building, so that mothers can drop in to see their children during their breaks. These centers are relatively large (eighty to one hundred children on the average), with well-qualified and well-paid staff. They are likely to offer the full range of services: education, recreation, and health care in a bright, cheerful, and well-equipped physical setting. The characteristics of the company may carry over to the center. For example, hygiene may be particularly stressed in a hospital daycare center, assembly-line routines—"all line up for juice now" or "you powder, I'll pin"—in a factory.

Cooperative centers. In private cooperative centers parents do a major part of the care, maintenance, and decision making, usually with the guidance of a paid director and some teachers. Fees are lower as a result of this in-kind service, but cooperative centers usually attract high-income families because the parents must have some flexibility in their work schedules to fit in their time at the center. These centers usually stress education and ideology rather than equipment, food, or health services.

Public service centers. Nine percent of the daycare centers in the United States receive government funding. They offer the widest range of services, from meals to medical attention, from toys to transportation, and all meet standards to insure adequate physical facilities, equipment, staff, and educational programs. There is usually an emphasis on children's cognitive development in an environment offering books, music, blocks, sand, paints, puzzles, lessons, and conversation. In Britain, public day nurseries give priority to single mothers who must work; in the United States eligibility is restricted to low-income families. The parents are often involved in policy making and may participate in auxiliary educational programs. The center staff may include student aides, community volunteers, and senior citizens as well as trained teachers and directors.

Research centers. This category includes only a tiny fraction of existing daycare centers, but it is a significant fraction because much of the research on daycare effects has been done in this kind of facility. These centers, usually affiliated with a university, reflect what is currently thought to be optimal daycare practice. The physical environment is spacious and stimulating. The educational curriculum is based on the latest in child development research as well as tried and true traditional nursery school activities. Their focus is usually language and intellectual development. The staff is ample, often experienced, and extensively trained in child development. They meet regularly with the researchers to talk about the program and the children. Teachers also make an effort to talk regularly with the parents, who tend to be from low-income families. Classes are small, and an effort is usually made to keep children with the same caregiver and classmates while they are in the program.

PART-TIME ARRANGEMENTS

Sometimes working mothers can adjust their schedules so that they need only part-time daycare. Sometimes they use a combination of arrangements. In these cases, nursery schools and playgroups can serve as daycare settings.

Nursery schools and nursery classes. In the United Kingdom 9 percent of the eligible three-year-olds and 33 percent of the four-year-olds are in nursery schools or classes; in the United States it is 26 percent of the three-year-olds and 48 percent of the four-year-olds. As we have seen, nursery schools tend to be for the relatively af-fluent. They were not originally designed to serve the needs of fulltime working mothers, and most offer morning programs only. Recently, however, accompanying the increased need for daycare, there have been adjustments. Some nursery schools now offer an extended day (from 9 to 2:30 rather than 9 to 12); others have joined with day nurseries to offer combined daycare/nursery school services. Traditionally, nursery schools have been concerned with children's creative expression and social adjustment and have offered children an opportunity for enriched play as they choose freely from a lavish buffet of blocks, dolls, dressups, puzzles, books, paints, and pets, with assistance, advice, comfort, or instruction provided by the teacher as needed. In the last fifteen years many nursery schools have also shifted to a more developmental curriculum, rather than simply providing these opportunities for free expression and exploration. Montessori nursery schools, which were always more oriented toward cognitive development, have also increased in popularity. In the United Kingdom there are both nursery schools and nursery classes in primary schools. Nursery schools are larger and have more materials, and children in them spend more time working alone on academic activities than children in nursery classes; children in nursery classes interact more with peers and do more dramatic play.[10] But both schools and classes are more likely to have good space, trained teachers, structured materials, and educational curricula than other kinds of center care.

Playgroups. In the United States playgroups are informal and irregular get-togethers of a few mothers and tots, usually in one of their homes, every week or so. Their purpose is purely social contact for mothers and children, not real daycare. In Great Britain playgroups are more formal, regular, and organized. They vary in size from six to forty children (usually not more than twenty per session), and meet for two to three hours several times a week in a house or, more often, a public hall. They are run by play leaders trained by the Preschool Playgroup Association. Often these are mothers. Playgroups appeal to middle-class mothers who have time to help in the group activities, raise funds, and repair equipment.

The playgroup offers children enriching experiences but not deliberate instruction or stimulation. There are more adult-led group activities like games, singing, stories, and art than in nursery schools, and not as much time for free interaction among the children.

These are the childcare arrangements being made by British and American mothers today. But what are the effects of the different arrangements on the children themselves?

5 / Child Development

Social scientists have been studying the effects of daycare on children's development for about fifteen years. Their usual method is to locate two groups of children—those attending a daycare center and those not attending one—and then to compare how well the two groups do on some test. If the average score on the test for the group of children in daycare is higher than the average score for the children not in daycare, it is concluded that daycare has a positive effect on development; if it is lower, then daycare is damaging. This is a very simple study, far too simple to do justice to the complex question of daycare effects. Consequently, although a consistent pattern does seem to emerge from the results of all the studies done so far, the reader should be aware of some of the limitations in this research.

First, only a limited number of daycare centers have been studied. Often they have been university-based, well-funded, and well-run centers that reflect what we think of as the best possible daycare. We don't know much about the quality of the other centers studied because the researchers have not observed children's experiences there or compared the performance of children from different centers. One might assume that community center directors who would agree to participate in a study would be proud of their centers and offer relatively good daycare; and so, again, the results reported probably apply to better-than-average daycare. We don't know the effects of worse-than-average daycare.

Regardless of the quality of the care, it is essential in any research on daycare effects to make sure that the groups being compared are identical in every way except in the one thing being studied: being in daycare. Meeting this seemingly obvious condition has been a problem for researchers. For one thing, they don't always know much about the experiences of children in the nondaycare group. Although these children have not been in a center at the time of the study, they may have had daycare-like experiences in a playgroup, nursery school, or with a babysitter. This could reduce apparent differences between the daycare and the nondaycare children. For another thing, although the researcher can pick children for the two groups who are the same age, whose families have comparable incomes, and who live in the same neighborhood, it is not possible to rule out other differences between the families that choose to use daycare and those that don't (such as mother's work status and attitude). Ideally, in a scientific study, the researcher would assign one group of children to daycare and the other to stay at home on a random basis. But this has only been done in two studies of daycare,[1] using nonworking, welfare mothers. It is not likely that many self-supporting parents would be willing to have their work status or their child's care determined by the random roll of a researcher's dice. Because families make their own choices about work and childcare, and thus "self-select" themselves into daycare or nondaycare groups, it is not possible to say with certainty that the differences observed between daycare and parent-care children are *caused* by daycare. There may also be differences in the experiences these children have at home that would make them different. This places further limitations on the findings that supposedly reflect daycare "effects."

Another limitation comes from the imprecision of our instruments for measuring differences between children. Our tools for assessing differences in children's development are very primitive. There is no available yardstick (or meter stick) for evaluating precisely children's social, emotional, and intellectual growth. We can make rough estimates, but these may miss subtle and important distinctions between children.

One tool used for getting such estimates is the standard intelligence or IQ test. In the preschool period this test measures children's abilities to use and understand language (words, concepts, or stories) and to manipulate and organize materials (putting pegs in holes, matching geometric figures, or copying complex designs with blocks). The child's score on such a test can then be compared to national norms for children's scores. This measure does tell us something important about how the child is progressing—in particular by the time the child is three or four years old, it gives a reasonably good prediction of how well the child is likely to do in school—but it does not indicate anything about the child's social skills, emotional development, or practical competence. Our measures of these qualities are more shaky. Keeping in mind all these limitations, what do the reasearchers have to say?

PHYSICAL HEALTH AND DEVELOPMENT

The child's physical development is the least difficult aspect of development to assess. We can at least see and agree on whether the child has a cold or can climb stairs. A number of studies of daycare effects have therefore used pediatricians', teachers', and mothers' reports on children's physical well-being and standard tests of children's motor abilities (walking, jumping, throwing a ball, handling tools) to find out whether children in daycare differ in these ways from children who stay at home with their mothers. Their findings are quite consistent. For children from poor families, daycare (in either university-based or community facilities) advances motor development and activity, increases height and weight faster, and decreases the likelihood of pediatric problems (from 50 percent to 23 percent, in one study).[2] For physical growth, daycare centers and daycare homes both have these advantages; for motor development, the benefit occurs only in centers. This probably comes from the fact that daycare centers offer better food, safety, health services, and opportunities for supervised exercise with lots of space, equipment, and other children than these children would receive at home.

On the other hand, if children already come from families and homes that provide these opportunities, no benefit in physical development accrues from going to even an excellent daycare center. There is no difference between middle-class children in daycare or parent care in height, motor skills, or activity.[3] There is, however, a difference in health. Children in daycare centers get more flu, rashes, colds, and coughs than children at home.[4] They catch everything that is going around, even if they are from the best of homes and even if they are in the best of daycare centers.

INTELLECTUAL DEVELOPMENT

A child's runny nose may be a price mothers are willing to pay to have their children in a daycare center while they work—especially if most of the wiping of that nose is done by the daycare staff—but what about the child's intellectual growth? Is daycare detrimental, as some have feared? This has been a question of concern and the focus of over thirty different studies in the last fifteen years.

The good news from all these studies—in Canada, England, Sweden, Czechoslovakia, the United States—is that care in a decent daycare facility has no apparent detrimental effects on children's intellectual development. Only one of these studies found that scores on tests of perception, language, and intelligence were lower for children attending a daycare center than for children of comparable family backgrounds being cared for by parents at home.[5] The two-year-olds in this study had been in daycare since they were less than eight weeks old, and the centers they attended met only minimal standards. Adult-child ratios in these centers ranged from 1:16 to 1:24, for example, and care was custodial at best. With this one exception, studies have shown that children in daycare centers do at least as well as children at home, and often they do better.[6] This was true not only in daycare centers at Harvard, the University of North Carolina, or Syracuse University, but also in community centers in New York, Chicago, Toronto, Boston, and Stockholm. Children in these centers have been found to do better in tests of verbal fluency, memory, and comprehension; they have been observed to copy designs made with blocks, solve problems, string beads, write their names, and draw circles, squares, and triangles earlier than children at home. Their speech is more complex, and they are able to identify other people's feelings and points of view earlier. On IQ tests there may be a difference of as much as 20 to 30 points between daycare and parent-care groups. Mothers of children in centers corroborate these results, reporting that daycare teaches children things they wouldn't have learned at home—concepts, arithmetic, practical skills. (The only thing the mothers complain about is that their children also pick up more bad language.[7])

This apparent advantage of daycare center attendance occurs most often for children aged two to four years who are from poor families, although differences for middle-class children have also been observed in some studies. The gains in intellectual development increase for the first couple of years that the child is in the center, but daycare children do not necessarily stay ahead of nondaycare children. Unless these children are in very inadequate homes or schools, when nondaycare children get to kindergarten or first grade they soon catch up to their daycare peers.[8] What daycare seems to do is to speed up children's intellectual development during the preschool period rather than to change it permanently.

The same kinds of results have been obtained in studies of differences between children who go to nursery schools and those who do not.[9] At the beginning of first grade, children from middle-class families who have been to nursery school are better able to manage on their own, know more about their environment, ask more questions; they are more ingenious with materials, have richer vocabularies, are more verbally expressive. Their peers as well as their teachers think they have better ideas and do better work. Similar differences in intellectual performance have been observed for poor children who attend model preschool programs.[10] Thus it seems that participation in a preschool program, daycare center, or nursery school, even part-time, can have at least temporary benefits for children's intellectual development.

But the same acceleration has not usually been observed for children in daycare homes or with babysitters. Although some studies have found no significant difference between children in homes and centers, when there *is* a difference in intellectual development, it always favors center daycare over home daycare.[11] Children with a daycare home provider, childminder, or babysitter, it seems, do about the same as children at home with their mothers, while children in daycare centers generally do better. In the New York Infant Day Care Study, for example, a study of some four hundred children from lower-income families attending eleven community daycare centers and one hundred daycare homes, of which most were in supervised daycare networks, children in centers and homes started off at six to twelve months getting about the same scores on standard intelligence tests.[12] They stayed at the same level through their second year, but by three years of age the scores of children in daycare homes had dropped to a significantly lower level than those of children in centers, and were at the same level as those of children who were at home with parents.

Another recent study that I directed, the Chicago Study of Child Care and Development, looked at one hundred and fifty two- to four-year-old children from a mixture of home backgrounds and a variety of care arrangements, including home with parents or babysitters, in daycare homes, in nursery schools, in daycare centers, and in combined nursery school/babysitter arrangements.[13] All these childcare arrangements occurred naturally in the community; they were not in exceptionally good or model daycare facilities. The children were tested on their abilities to understand sentences, to name colors, fruits, and animals, to remember numbers, to identify photographs of objects, to use play materials, to solve problems, to label pictures of emotional situations, to copy designs made with blocks, to visualize how things would look to another person, and to communicate with a listener. On all these measures of intellectual competence, a clear difference was found between children in home care (with parents, sitter, or daycare home provider) and center care (in nursery school, daycare center, or combined center and sitter), favoring those in center care. This occurred for children of all family backgrounds, for both boys and girls, after as little as six months in daycare.

In sum, it appears likely that there is something about daycare centers and nursery schools that stimulates or maintains children's intellectual development, at least until the beginning of school. Remember, however, that these findings—however positive they are about daycare—do not guarantee that all children will benefit from being in a center. The centers that had these apparent advantages, though not all "exceptional," were all of relatively good quality; poor-quality centers would not be expected to have such positive outcomes. The children who were most likely to benefit from daycare centers came from relatively poor families; children from affluent families did not gain so much. The measures of intellectual development used were of an academically oriented sort: language skills, manipulative abilities, perceptual abilities. Children from homes might possibly do better than children in centers on tests of more practical competencies (buying a loaf of bread, getting to the store, and such). Although centers in these studies were superior to homes for supporting children's intellectual development, this does not mean that the same kinds of benefit might not be possible in homes; these studies only dealt with averages, not individual facilities or children. Some children might do better in a home setting than they would in a center; some homes undoubtedly provide more intellectual stimulation than many centers.

RELATIONS WITH MOTHER

Children's social relations are at the core of the controversy over daycare. Opponents fear that children in daycare will be deprived of their proper relations with their mothers and will become the pawns of their peers. Advocates claim that children in daycare will be appropriately independent of their mothers' apron strings and become more socially competent with their peers. Researchers have tried to determine which, if either, of these outcomes is likely.

Over the course of the first year of life, every home-reared infant in a normal family develops a strong emotional feeling for the person who cares for him, plays with him, and loves him. This feeling of attachment distinguishes the focal caregiver-playmate from other more casual social companions. The child wants to be near this person, especially in times of stress, fatigue, or illness, to hold and be held by her, to keep her in his view or at least at his beck and call. He prefers her company and contact to anyone else's. If they must be separated, he is often distressed when she leaves. This fond feeling becomes obvious by the end of the first year and continues to be evident over the next several years. Most often, the first object of the child's affection is the mother. If a father or an older sibling is centrally involved in the child's life, the child soon develops attachments to these people too.

Researchers have struggled to develop ways of assessing this feeling of attachment. Needless to say, the task has been very challenging. There is no thermometer for love. The best solution devised so far involves placing the child in a mildly stressful situation—alone in an unfamiliar room with an unfamiliar woman—and observing his reactions to his mother's leaving and returning. Some children in this situation cling to their mothers and won't even let them leave the room. Other children ignore their mother's departure. They continue playing with toys or the stranger, and when the mother returns, they actively avoid her. Still other children are ambivalent in their reactions—clinging to their mother one moment and spurning her the next. Most children show a balanced pattern that has been called "secure attachment." They are able to leave the mother's side to explore the toys and the room, but they clearly prefer to be with her than to be with the stranger, and as the mother begins her comings and goings at the researcher's request, they show more and more concern and are more likely to stay close to her. They always greet her enthusiastically when she returns.

This test situation may not be the perfect solution to the assessment of attachment, but it does give a measure that is quite easy to assess, relatively constant over time, and related to the child's behavior to the mother at home. It has been used in a number of studies of daycare to try to find out whether children in daycare still form attachments to their mothers, and, if so, whether they are the same kind of attachments as those of children who are being raised exclusively by their mothers. This assessment situation has also been used to find out what kind of relationship these children form with the caregivers who look after them.

The findings from these studies indicate unequivocally that children in daycare are indeed attached to their mothers and that this feeling is not replaced by their relation with another caregiver.[14] They may also form an affectionate relationship with a childminder who is involved in their care for a substantial period of time, and this caregiver is preferred to a stranger, but daycare children still overwhelmingly prefer their mothers to this caregiver. They go to their mother for help, stay close to her, approach her more often, interact with her more, and go to her rather than the caregiver when distressed or bored.[15] In the daycare center they do not greet the teacher in the morning with the same joy as they greet the mother at night. They do not behave as if the caregiver is a substitute mother, nor is this how caregivers perceive themselves.

But are there any differences in the quality of the relationship with their mother for children who are away from her every day? On many measures of children's attachment to their mother, no differences between daycare and maternal-care children have been found. Although daycare children are undoubtedly more used to separations from their mothers, and although they don't usually protest when their mothers leave them in the daycare setting[16] just as maternal-care children don't protest separations at home, they are just as likely to be upset when their mothers leave them in the unfamiliar setting. They are just as likely to be angry or ambivalent toward their mother. They can still be classified as "securely attached." There is only one way in which daycare children consistently differ from maternal-care children: in the physical distance or closeness they seek out with mothers. In the unfamiliar setting of the laboratory where so many studies were made, daycare children did not go to or stay as close to their mothers as maternal-care children did, nor did they seek as much physical contact, and they were more likely to ignore the mother when she came back into the room after a brief separation.[17]

What does this difference mean? Some think it represents a disturbance in the child's relationship with the mother, since usually children in "traditional" maternal-care families who act this way also tend to be less well adjusted. For daycare children, however, it seems more plausible that this greater distance represents an earlier or adaptive independence from the mother that is a natural and realistic response to daily separations from her and regular interactions with stangers. For daycare children, this pattern of greater distance is related to greater overall social competence, not to poorer adjustment. What is more, although these daycare children maintain greater physical distance from their mother, they are just as affectionate with her—or more so. Their relationship is just not so intensely physical.

The difference in independence or intensity of the mother-child relationship is most marked if children begin daycare in the first year of life, before their attachment relationship with mother has totally formed. It is also more likely to occur if they are in a daycare center than in a daycare home or with a babysitter (although greater independence from mother has also been observed in these arrangements) and if they are in fulltime care rather than part-time. When, in addition to the child's being in daycare, the mother is inaccessible and insensitive, this can push independence to an unhealthy extreme. Independence does not seem to be affected by the quality of daycare, however; it has been observed in both exceptional and ordinary daycare.

RELATIONS WITH PEERS

Preschool children progress in interacting with their peers from simply staring to approaching and exploring, to smiling and offering toys, to interactions that are intense, contingent, and reciprocal, to complex games, role play, and cooperative activities in groups. They learn to make friends and they acquire "enemies."

A large number of researchers have focused on daycare children's relations with their peers, expecting that since these children have so much more experience with other children, this must make a difference in their social relations with agemates. They have observed children in their daycare settings as they interact with peers after greater or lesser amounts of time in daycare. They have brought unacquainted pairs of children who are in either daycare or parental care into a set-up play situation in the laboratory and watched their interactions with one another. They have tested children from different care arrangements on their willingness to cooperate and help each other. The results of their studies suggest that daycare does indeed make a difference in peer relations.[18]

Although daycare and parent-care children do not differ in the kinds of interactions they have with familiar friends or playmates, with unacquainted peers daycare children are more at ease socially. In all these test situations, children attending daycare centers or nursery schools are more outgoing, less timid and fearful, more helpful and cooperative than children who are being raised at home. Their interactions with peers are also more complex, reciprocal, and mature. This social advance may not always look positive, however. Daycare center children are not only more outgoing but they are more likely to be loud, boisterous, competitive, and aggressive with their peers. Parents may be concerned about this apparent negative effect. Still it seems likely that the difference reflects greater maturity and social competence rather than being something to worry about, since this is something that goes along with increasing maturity in this age period and, as we shall see, is accompanied by other indications of social competence.

Social competence has been assessed in a variety of

ways, in natural observations and standard situations, and always, where there is a difference, it is consistently the children in daycare who seem more advanced.[19] Daycare children are more self-confident, assured, and assertive in unfamiliar test situations. They act more at ease and are more likely to admit to an examiner that they don't know the answer to a test question. They are more self-sufficient and independent of parents and teachers. They can make their own choices, dress themselves, and brush their own hair at a younger age. Yet they are also more cooperative and helpful to parent, teacher, or examiner when the situation requires it. They are more verbally expressive and knowledgeable about the social world. For example, they know what activities and toys are considered appropriate for boys and girls earlier than home-care children do. They act in less stereotyped and more original ways. They can competently show a stranger around their home, get her a glass of water, and show her their toys. When they start school, they are better adjusted, more persistent at their tasks, and more likely to be leaders. Again, there are apparent drawbacks. The daycare children may also be less polite and agreeable, less repectful of others' rights, and less responsive to adult requests. Nevertheless, by all these indications, their social skills are advanced over those of agemates who remain at home with parents. It's not that they are simply more friendly (which might be expected from so much experience with people outside the family), but that they are more socially mature.

Are these effects permanent? The longer the child is in daycare, at least up to a couple of years, the stronger the effects are. They seem to carry over into the first few school grades, but then the differences between daycare children and parent-care children decrease. As with the differences in intellectual development favoring children in daycare, the positive effects have been observed more often for children in daycare centers and nursery schools than for children in daycare homes or with babysitters. In one study where mothers were interviewed, increased self-reliance by their children as a result of their daycare experience was mentioned by 60 percent of the mothers with children in daycare centers, 50 percent of mothers with children in daycare homes, and 11 percent of mothers with children with babysitters.[20]

What is it, then, about daycare experience in centers and nursery schools that might cause these differences in children's social and intellectual competence?

6 / Programs, Places, Peers

Why do some types of daycare seem to accelerate children's development of independence, knowledge, and social competence? What is it about particular daycare settings that facilitates development? Let us look at three different aspects of daycare that could be responsible; the educational program or curriculum, the physical space and equipment, and the presence of other children.

PROGRAMS

An educational curriculum is one critical factor that distinguishes most daycare centers and nursery schools from most homes (daycare and the child's own). Although certainly many centers are merely custodial and many homes do offer a rich diet of intellectual and social stimulation, for the most part it is in daycare centers and nursery schools that one finds children involved in formal educational activities.

Open and closed. In research comparing different daycare centers, it has been found that any educational program is better for children's learning and development than no educational program at all.[1] But the kind of educational program matters even more. In one kind of program the teacher is very controlling, directive, and didactic. She tells the children what to do and when to do it. She gives the children clear and explicit lessons, according to a strict schedule. This program has been called by various names: structured, closed, or formal. At the other extreme is the kind of program where the teacher is unintrusive and indirect. She prepares material and activities for the children but then lets them choose from among them, going at their own pace, following their own interests, and making discoveries about the social and physical world on their own. She guides, encourages, and helps the children in their activities but she does not exhort, direct, instruct, or restrict them. This program, by contrast, has been called unstructured, open, or informal.

In a closed program, the teacher controls what happens and insures that what is intended actually occurs. She makes clear to the children (and often their parents) her goals and expectations about what is right for the child to do. Her behavior is consistent and predictable. An open program may be more chaotic because the teacher is not in direct control. Her behavior and that of the children are variable. Closed programs provide clear limits and structured instruction, but lack opportunities for autonomy, initiative, and one-to-one interaction with the teacher or other children. Open programs offer varied activities, opportunities for rewarding contact with peers, freedom to explore, and the chance to make choices and decisions; adult input and engagement are low.

As might be expected, these two very different kinds of programs have distinctly different effects on children's behavior. A number of studies have compared children in open and closed programs in preschool classes and the primary grades.[2] In closed programs children show less independence, less cooperation, less initiative, less helping, less imaginative play, less play with peers, less physical activity, and less aggression; their activities are more purposeful and task-oriented. In open classrooms children do more functional and imaginative play with peers, more independent work, more work and helping with another child; they are more likely to persist on a task, talk about it, and ask questions. The two different kinds of program are reflected not only in children's behavior in the classroom itself but in their performance on tests outside the classroom. Children in closed programs do better on intelligence and achievement tests; children in open programs do better on tests of curiosity, inventiveness, and problem solving.

In the real world, not all programs are at one extreme or the other; many, perhaps most, are somewhere in between. They offer some prescribed, structured activities or lessons at some time during the day, but also give children frequent opportunities for free play and free choices. In one study of nursery schools, nursery classes, and playgroups in Great Britain and the United States by Kathy Sylva and her colleagues,[3] programs offering a moderate number of structured activities were found to be ideal. In programs with just two structured educational activities per half-day session, children were observed to play constructively with the prescribed task materials even after the structured activity was completed. Their play was more elaborate and included more complex, cognitively worthwhile and challenging actions (such as building, drawing, doing puzzles) than that of children in either more closed programs with a greater number of prescribed lessons and tasks or more open programs with no prescribed activities. Prescribing tasks, these investigators concluded, can promote children's concentration and imagination by helping them sustain attention and master new skills. It can also, if taken to an extreme, become too restricting. Their recommendation for an optimal curriculum is "a basic diet of free choice punctuated lightly by prescribed educational tasks."

Teachers agree,[4] and so do the results of other studies.[5] Children in classes with the greatest number of structured activities (drills) had low gains in cognitive abilities; children in classes with no structured activities had no gains in creativity or achievement. With moderate structure and some room for child initiative, children gained in cognition, achievement, and creativity; they were also highest in self-esteem.

The amount of structure in a program is usually combined with another program dimension, the educational content and goals. Closed programs are more likely to emphasize language, prereading, manipulation of objects, and other intellectual and academic skills; open programs are more likely to give priority to children's enjoyment, self-expression, creativity, and sociability. Again, most programs are somewhere in between these two extremes.

Combinations. One major study of preschool programs compared the effects of programs that differed in the amount of structure and the goals of the curriculum. The researchers, Louise Miller and Jean Dyer, set up a number of model preschool programs in four different schools that catered to low-income families.[6] Then they observed the behavior of teachers and children in these programs and tested the children's development throughout the school term and three years later.

The direct instruction program they set up (modeled after the "Distar" curriculum of Sigfried Engelmann, Carl Bereiter, and Wesley Becker) was highly structured and totally academic. Every day a teacher directed youngsters in small groups of five or six in three twenty-minute lessons on reading, language, and arithmetic. The lessons were controlled completely by the teacher, according to a script she was given by the program designers. She modeled, corrected, and rewarded children's responses in a fast-paced, loud, repetitive drill of short questions and answers.

> Teacher: This is a *wheel* (shows picture).
> Child: Wheel.
> Teacher: Good. It is a wheel. Let's all say it. This is a wheel.
> Children: This is a wheel.
> Teacher: Again.
> Children: This is a wheel.
> Teacher: Let's say it one more time . . .

Children in this direct instruction program gained more rapidly on tests of intelligence, and by the end of the preschool year they scored highest of any program in arithmetic, sentence production, vocabulary, and persistence on a difficult task. Three years later, however, at the end of second grade in a non-Distar class, these children were low on tests of IQ, letters, numbers, word meanings, inventiveness, and curiosity. Their preschool gains had completely disappeared.

Another structured, academically oriented program set up in this study was modeled after the DARCEE (Demonstration and Research Center for Early Education) program in Nashville, Tennessee. This was a program designed to improve children's language skills and attitudes toward school. Like Distar, it included intensive teacher instruction, small groups, and formal academic lessons. But the lessons were not simply repetitions of verbal patterns, as in Distar; they included playing table games, copying designs, and identifying letters and numbers. There were both formal and informal conversations between children and teachers, often one to one, and children were given free choices as well as prescribed lessons. This program was only "moderately" structured. In the testings, children in the DARCEE programs also gained rapidly on IQ tests—they had the highest scores of any group after eight weeks—and tests of arithmetic, vocabulary, sentence production, and persistence, but, unlike the Distar children, they gained as well in curiosity, inventiveness, and social participation. Unlike the highly structured and academic Distar program, then, the moderately structured and more comprehensive DARCEE program had positive social-emotional outcomes as well as intellectual ones. What is more, the children in the DARCEE program continued to be high on IQ, inventiveness, curiosity, and verbal-social skills at the end of the second grade.

In the model Montessori program also set up by Miller and Dyer, the materials were structured but the schedule was open. Children were free to select whatever materials interested them and to work on them at their own pace, with little teacher interference. The teacher introduced the materials at what she thought were appropriate times, and kept records of children's use and progress with the materials, but gave no lessons in how to use them. Montessori materials themselves are "self-correcting." There is only one right way to build a tower with the Montessori graduated cylinders or to make the pink staircase, for example. The content emphasized by the Montessori program is intellectual (prereading, sensory discrimination, concepts of size and weight). In the standard assessments children in this program excelled in curiosity and inventiveness at the end of the program school year, but

three years later they were not only high in these qualities but also high in IQ, reading, and mathematics and
were more highly motivated to achieve in school. Again,
the benefits of another example of a moderately structured program are demonstrated.

The most open and also the most socially oriented
program in Miller's and Dyer's study was the so-called
traditional nursery school program. This program was
child-centered and slow-paced. Most of the time children
engaged in free play, choosing from make-believe, dressups, physical activities, puzzles, books, and science materials. At other times they had group activities such as
singing, stories, and field trips. The teachers exerted no
pressure; they were warm and accepting; the children
were free to do whatever interested them. The goal of the
program was happy children who were curious, self-motivated, and sociable. At the end of a year in this program, the children met the goals of the program; they had
more curiosity and were more active socially. But they
were also more aggressive and not as likely to do well in
intelligence tests. Three years later, they were still high
on verbal-social skills such as cooperation and initiating
conversations but, as earlier, low in academic achievement.

In sum, the results of studies comparing different kinds
of educational programs in preschool centers are consistent in pointing up the benefits—for constructive activity,
for intelligence, for later achievement, for positive moti-
vation, persistence, and problem solving, and for social
skills—of a preschool program that blends prescribed
educational activities with opportunities for free choice,
that has some structure, but also allows children to explore a rich environment of objects and peers on their
own without teacher direction.

PLACES

What children remember most about daycare is the physical experience—the discomfort of lying quietly on their backs at naptime, of not being able to get a swing, of digging in the sand, of eating outdoors on the grass.[7] The experience of daycare is a very sensual one, and we might expect that differences in the physical setting would also affect children's behavior and development. Certainly the physical settings of daycare centers and homes are dramatically different, and this may be part of the reason we find differences in children's development in these two types of care arrangement.

Space. Researchers have investigated the effects of variation in space, equipment, and materials in daycare settings in an attempt to find out how children's behavior and development are influenced by the physical setting. Space, it turns out, is related both to the size of the classroom and to the number of children in the class. The usual measure of space, therefore, is not simply the total space in the setting but the space per child. Several researchers have set up experimental playgroups in different-sized classrooms, allowing, for example, 15, 25, 50, or 75 square feet per child. When the space per child is very limited (less than 25 square feet), these studies show, children become more physical and aggressive with their peers, more destructive with their toys; they spend more time climbing or doing nothing, and less time running, jumping, chasing, and interacting socially.[8] In the United States, licensing standards for daycare centers and daycare homes ensure space that exceeds this limit of crowding (more than 35 square feet per child). Therefore, space is probably not a major influence on the development of children in most daycare settings, at least in those that meet licensing requirements.[9]

What may be more important is the way that space is organized. A spatial organization that allows children privacy and quiet, where different kinds of activities—loud block play and quiet puzzle play, or messy finger painting and neat pine-cone collecting—are kept clearly separated, may be more beneficial than simply more square feet of play area.

Materials. The materials that go into the separate activity areas can also be important. Different kinds of behavior obviously are typical for different play areas. Outdoors, with playground equipment, children do more running, playing, laughing, rough and tumble play; they are less aggressive, more mature, cooperative, and sociable; they talk more to peers than to teachers, and play lengthy, complex games. Indoors, in the dramatic play area (dressups and dolls), children also talk among themselves and have complex social interactions. In the building-construction area (blocks and boards), they talk less—except for quarrels—but their play is complex, rich, and challenging. In the art and academic areas (paints and puzzles), their play is complex and they use the materials constructively, but involvement with these materials is more likely to be accompanied by interaction with the teacher than is involvement with blocks, boards, dolls, or dressups. With materials for "messing around" (sand, clay, buttons, and assorted junk), their activities, often with other children, are creative and experimental but somewhat less complex. Small toys also bring out less complex behaviors as children do what the toys suggest: with toy guns they behave aggressively; with checkers and pickup sticks they interact socially;

with gyroscopes and microscopes they play alone. If there are no materials available and the equipment is fixed, inflexible, or limited, children spend their time watching, waiting, cruising, touching, imitating, chatting, quarreling, and horsing around with peers; their play is of a very low complexity and intellectual value.[10]

The complexity and intensity of children's involvement with materials is also influenced by the number of activities each play area offers. Good play areas have four or five things for each child to do. For example, in the sandbox there is not only sand but shovels, pails, water, and a dump truck; the doll corner has not only dolls but doll clothes, furniture, and a house. A more plentiful supply of materials leads to more cooperative, constructive, and relevant participation and less conflict.[11]

Overall quality. Space of good physical quality can be found in homes or centers, although materials that elicit high-level constructive play (puzzles, blocks, art) may be more likely in centers, with opportunities for free play and tactile exploration (water, sand, dough, pillows) more likely in homes. In either kind of setting, the quality of the physical space affects the adults' behavior as well as the children's. In daycare settings where the physical equipment and space are varied, accessible, complex, and offer children lots to do and lots of choices, not only are children more involved but caregivers are more sensitive, friendly, and interactive.[12] It is this combination of good materials and space and responsive caregiver behavior that is the best predictor of positive outcomes for children. Just having more numerous or more exotic toys and playthings in a home or center does not guarantee developmental gains.[13] In one study, cameras, puppets, and tape recorders were added to four-year-olds' daycare classes—with no apparent effects on the children's intellectual development. If their teachers had been trained in how to best utilize these materials, and had interacted with the children using them in these ways, some benefits might have occurred. In physical settings of good quality, caregivers can both allow children freedom to explore and spend their time demonstrating constructive activities with the materials available, rather than supervising and scolding all the time.

PEERS

One reason many parents choose group daycare for their children, send them to nursery school, or join a playgroup is for the experience the children will gain from playing with others their own age. These parents hope and expect that their children will become more socially skilled, will learn to share, cooperate, make friends, and compete without being aggressive, and perhaps will learn more mature behaviors from their peers. Given the availability of peers in daycare centers and nursery schools and the fact, as we saw in the last chapter, that children attending these centers are more socially and intellectually advanced, this assumption is not unrealistic. Peers can be models, tutors, behavior modifiers, competitive partners, and congenial and cooperative playmates. Only children do certain things together, such as using the teeter-totter, playing with a jack-in-the-box, jumping off a platform twenty times, or playing peek-a-boo under a blanket. Play with another child, it has been found, is more complex and cognitively challenging than play alone.[14] The important question for us is how experience with other children in daycare fosters children's social and intellectual skills. Is it simply exposure to any other children? Is it experience with lots of children? Is it playing with many different kinds of children? Is it participating with children in any kinds of activities or particular kinds?

One good friend. Studies have shown that with a familiar playmate (as opposed to an unfamiliar peer) children's social play is more interactive, cooperative, and connected; the pair stays closer together, smiles, imitates, and shares more; cries, frets, and takes away the other's toys less.[15] This suggests that experience with even one other peer might benefit the child by giving him the opportunity to practice the more advanced social skills that occur only with such a friend. A study by Jacqueline Becker with very young children (nine months old) tested whether the highly skilled interactions developed with a friend would generalize to an unfamiliar peer.[16] Pairs of first-born infants were brought together for ten one-hour play sessions in one of the children's homes. As the two children became friends, as in other studies, the frequency, complexity, and responsiveness of their interactions increased. On the eleventh visit, an unfamiliar child of the same age, who had not participated in this experience with a peer, came to visit. What happened showed that children who had had the experience did generalize their social skills to the visitor. They were more sociable and responsive, sustained interactions longer, and initiated more games than the inexperienced children. Another study, with older preschool children, showed the same thing.[17] Having a regular playmate was associated with more responsive and lengthy interactions with a peer stranger. So it seems that *any* experience with another child may be of value for the development of early social competence. The same may be true of intellectual development, since play observed between pairs of children is more cordial, complex, and intellectually worthwhile than play in which more than two or fewer than two children are involved.[18] While this is true, however, it cannot be the whole story, since we would not see the advantage we have noted for children in center as opposed to home daycare. Children in both settings are likely to have some experience with at least one other child.

Peer interaction: How much with how many? Is this difference because children in daycare centers have more experience with other children? This also seems unlikely, since several studies have shown that children in daycare homes, on the average, spend the same amount of time with other children as children in centers do.[19] The major difference between centers or nursery schools and other forms of care is not how much time children spend playing together, but the number of other children they play with. In the Chicago Study of Child Care and Development, an estimate of the average number of different children contacted during a two-hour period was two in home care with mother, three in home care with a babysitter or in a daycare home, eight in nursery school, and thirteen in a daycare center. It was found that the number of different children the child interacted with was positively related to development.

Does this mean, then, that the more children the child plays with the better? Probably not. For one thing, this finding does not mean that playing with more children caused the child's advanced development; it may be that more advanced children sought out or attracted more children to play with. For another thing, there are most likely limits to how many children it is beneficial to interact with, limits that were not exceeded in the care arrangements in this study. In the National Day Care Study, a massive study of sixty-four daycare centers and more than 3000 children in Atlanta, Detroit, and Seattle, it was found that children in large classes, having more than twenty children, did more poorly on tests and in their classroom interactions than those in smaller groups.[20] In large classes there was more crying, hostility, and apathy, less conversation, cooperation, reflection, innovation, and elaborate play. This finding has been supported in other studies, too, where class size has varied.[21] It seems that there is a maximum number of children in a daycare class (not exceeding seven for infants, eleven for toddlers, and eighteen for preschoolers) beyond which detrimental effects occur. In homes where there is only one caregiver, the maximum size should be smaller (not exceeding three for toddlers, according to the National Day Care Home Study).

The size of the class or daycare home group not only indicates something about the number of children the child is exposed to and is likely to interact with. It also implies something about the demands on the caregiver; large classes permit less time for each child. Even if the adult-child ratio is the same because there are two or three caregivers in the class, the higher noise level and increased hubbub of a larger class can be more physically and psychologically demanding for both teacher and child. Thus, even though it may be valuable for the child to play with many children, this does not mean that larger groups are better. They allow the child the opportunity to interact with more different children, but they deprive him of teacher attention, guidance, and responsiveness.

Variety of peers: Mix or match?   Children in daycare, as well as interacting with a larger number of children, also interact with a greater variety of different children than do children in home care. Perhaps this has some advantage for their development and social relations.

Among the kinds of variety that have been studied so far are sex and age. When both boys and girls are included in nursery school groups, girls have been observed to be more independent and boys more socially responsive and less disruptive than their peers in same-sex groups.[22] Both differences are in the direction of greater social competence for the children in mixed-sex groups. In mixed-age groups also, children have been observed to be more socially competent. They have more frequent and complex interactions with their peers and are more cooperative, persistent, flexible, and knowledgeable in tests of social competence and intelligence. The advantage is especially marked for the younger children in the mixed-age group.[23]

But this apparent benefit of interaction with different kinds of other children does not account for why children in daycare centers and nursery schools are more advanced than children in daycare homes, since the homes usually offer a mixture of ages and sexes. In daycare homes, in fact, according to the National Day Care Home Study, mixed ages is not necessarily advantageous for the child. For toddlers in mixed-age groups (with either infants or preschoolers), more time is spent alone, not interacting with either the caregiver or the other children; for preschoolers, if younger children are present, although more time is spent playing with the other children, less time is spent in appropriately stimulating interaction with the caregiver. What seems best in a home daycare situation is a relatively narrow age range of not more than two years. The same may be true in daycare centers and nursery schools as well; in the studies documenting the advantages of mixed-age groups, the age range in the mixed classes did not exceed two or three years.

The issue of the influence of interacting with peers is a complex one. Experience with one other peer seems to be better than experience with none; experience with more different peers is probably better than experience with one—at least up to a certain point; experience with too many peers in the same class, or at the same time, may be detrimental. But what happens within the class or day-care setting, including how peers are grouped, depends on a very large extent on the last—but certainly not least—aspect of the daycare arrangement: the adult care-giver. Children's behavior in daycare depends on both interactions with peers and interactions with adults. Their development is affected not by just any experience with other children, but by experience with peers in the context of adult-guided activities. The importance of the caregiver underlies and complicates the effects of all three of the aspects of daycare we have discussed: she selects and administers the educational curriculum; she arranges the physical space and selects the equipment and materials; she divides the children into groups and supervises their social interaction. At the same time, her behavior is affected by the program, the physical space, and the number and kind of children. The caregiver is a pivotal figure.

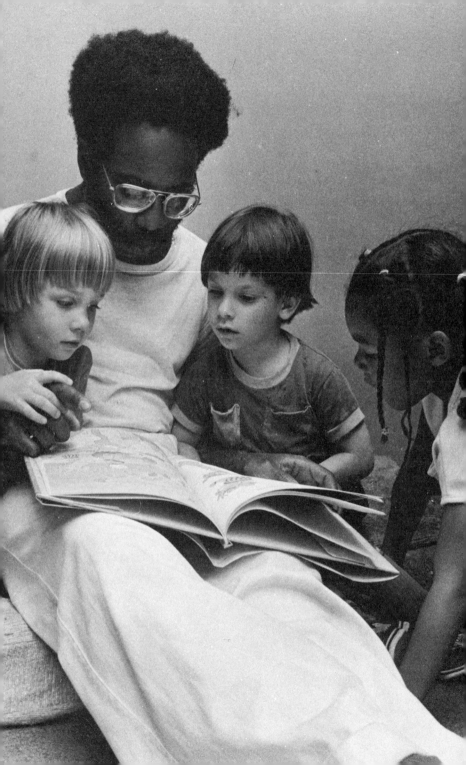

7 / Caregivers

The first caregiver is the parent. Over the past two decades, a substantial body of research has accumulated that looks into the effects of different styles of parental behavior on children's development. The observations and interviews that researchers have used to study parents and children suggest quite clearly that, although parents are not totally responsible for their children's development, they do have a substantial impact.[1]

The affection parents express, through close physical contact, nurturance, and sensitivity to the child's needs, is related to the child's feelings of security and affection toward the parents. When parents are consistently angry or rejecting to the child, the child rewards them with irritability, aggression, and emotional problems. When parents are affectionate and supportive, the child is happy and affectionate in return.

When the parent's affectionate or rejecting behavior is combined with other, managerial behaviors, its effect goes beyond the child's relation with the parent and his behavior at home; it affects the child's whole approach to life. When the parent is affectionate but uses strict, authoritarian discipline, the child has a strong likelihood of becoming dependent, polite, obedient, conforming, and compliant; when the parent is affectionate but lax and permissive in discipline, the child is likely to be active, outgoing, and creative, but perhaps immature. When the parent is rejecting, on the other hand, and this is combined with heavy-handed, restrictive discipline, the child will most likely be fearful, submissive, withdrawn, and dull. When parental rejection is accompanied by permissiveness, or by permissiveness at first and then strict discipline at a later age, the child is likely to be hostile, aggressive, and disobedient.

The optimal pattern of parental affection and discipline for encouraging children's independence and sociability is a balance somewhere in the middle of these extremes. It combines warmth and affection, nurturance and sensitivity, with a moderate amount of control. The parent sets firm limits for the child, but they are reasonable and not too numerous. Demands are consistent and given with rational explanations. Both social responsibility and independent autonomy are encouraged in the child. Children whose parents act toward them in this way have been observed to be friendly, cooperative, self-reliant, independent, and happy—not only at home, but in nursery school, daycare, and testing situations.

Two other parental qualities have also been found to affect children's development: stimulation and responsiveness. As early as six months, infants' perceptual and cognitive skills are related to the amount of time their mother has rocked, jiggled, talked to, and played with them, and this relation continues as the child gets older. The more the mother provides appropriate materials and arranges intellectual experiences, shares, expands, and elaborates the child's activities, focuses the child's attention on exploring objects, entertains and talks to the child—in brief, the more stimulating the quality of her interaction—the better the child performs in assessments of intelligence or intellectual development. Especially related to the child's intellectual development is the mother's verbal input. The more the mother talks to the child (at least within the range observed in most families), the better it is for the child's intellectual development. But mothers who talk a lot also modify their speech to the child so that it is responsive and appropriate. They use shorter, simpler, and more repetitive sentences than they would with an adult. They talk about objects and activities that the child is looking at or playing with. They accept the child's often painfully inadequate first efforts to speak, not intolerantly criticizing inadequacies.

The need for responsiveness starts early in the infant's life. It is important for the baby to learn that the world is in many ways a predictable place and that he can anticipate and to some extent control the people and things in it. To help the infant develop this general expectation, it is essential that parents interact with the infant not only frequently but in response to the specific signals and demands the baby makes. The timing and content of the interaction should not be at the parent's whim, but should mesh with the infant's needs, desires, interests, and schedule. Knowledge that when he cries someone comes to comfort or feed him, when he smiles, someone smiles back, when he reaches for a toy out of his grasp, someone gives it to him, encourages the child to explore new situations and new people and promotes his development and confidence. Later, in the preschool years, responding to the child's interests, demands, questions, and expectations in ways that are appropriate and stimulating is one strategy for encouraging the child to continue to ask questions and to explore. Parents can also increase the likelihood that children will behave in particularly desirable ways (whether sitting quietly or feeding the puppy) by responding to these behaviors in positive ways when they occur. In sum, the parent's role includes being a dispenser of love and a disciplinarian, a verbal stimulator, a sensitive responder, a provider of materials, and a choreographer of experiences for the child.

One thing that limits our current knowledge about the effects of parental behavior on children's development is that until very recently most studies focused on mothers and ignored fathers. This situation is being remedied now, and research suggests that the father contributes to the child's development in somewhat different ways from the mother. While his role in providing affection and discipline may parallel hers, the father is more likely to be a special playmate, who engages in exciting, physical games and active rough and tumble fun. This contributes to the child's sociability. He also provides psychological support for the mother and thus affects the child's development indirectly through her.

Another limitation in our knowledge about parents' influence on their children's development is the fact that much of our information about family patterns comes from relatively affluent, well-educated, middle-class families. In families where parents are poor and have little education, some studies show, behavior follows approximately the same patterns for the first year and a half of the child's life, but thereafter these parents are likely to be less affectionate, verbal, responsive, and consistent, and more restrictive and punitive. They talk to the children less and their conversations are less focused, complex, and didactic. These differences can be linked to a number of factors, one being how little these parents may know about child development. Mothers with more knowledge about child development, from books, courses, or training, have been observed to be more affectionate, talkative, playful, and responsive, to impose fewer restrictions, to do more teaching, and to stimulate the children more at appropriate levels.

Not only have studies on parental influence limited their domain to middle-class families; they have usually restricted their observations to "traditional" two-parent families where the father works and the mother stays home with the children. It is of interest to know whether these same effects occur when the mother is not the sole caregiver and the children are in daycare. It should be remembered that even if children spend 40 hours a week in daycare, that leaves 128 hours for them to be at home with their parents. How much does parental behavior affect children's development despite the fact that they are in daycare?

WORKING MOTHERS

Working mothers spend about the same amount of time in child-related activities as nonworking mothers do. But what about the quality of the time they spend with their children? Do working mothers try harder—attempting to compensate for leaving their children by offering them special times and treats—or does the working mother's exhaustion dull the quality of her interactions with her children? In observations of family interactions made at home at the end of the workday, working mothers have been observed to play and talk with their children more than nonworking mothers.[2] This suggests that they may indeed have special times with their children. But what we don't know is how frequent these special times are, or if all their interactions have this stimulating quality. In a "standard" situation, when mothers are asked to come to a room at the university and asked to play with their children, dress them, read to them, and such, or when mothers are asked questions about their behavior with their children, no differences have been found between working and nonworking mothers: the quality of their interactions with their children is the same.[3] What seems likely is that the end of the day is an especially social time for working mothers and their children, and not for mothers who are at home all day, but that at other times the quality of the interactions with their children would be very similar.

In the past some studies of children whose mothers were employed found that these children did not do as well on tests or in school as children of nonworking mothers, but these findings were not consistent. More recent studies that have investigated maternal satisfaction have found this to be a better prediction of mother-child interaction than work status alone. More important for the overall quality of interaction with their children than simply whether the mother works or not, these studies suggest, is how satisfied the mother is with her role as worker or homemaker. Satisfied women are consistently more warm, involved, playful, stimulating, and effective with their children than unsatisfied women.[4] And just as in the studies I have mentioned of childrearing in traditional families, children of working mothers who have these qualities appear to develop more competently. In one study by Ellen Hock, whether the mother was working full-time or part-time or not at all was not related to how well her baby did on tests or how close and secure the relationship between them was; but if a mother who was not working thought it was better to be working, or if a working mother thought she should be the baby's exclusive caregiver, the child's relations with mother were disturbed.[5] The children of these conflicted mothers were likely to respond to the mother's approaches with avoidance or crying. In another study it was again found that infants of mothers who were homemakers and preferred it that way were more sociable than those of discontented homemakers who wished they were working.[6] With older children, too, it has been found that the child's self-esteem and adjustment are higher when the mother is satisfied with her role as worker or housewife.[7]

In the most recent and carefully controlled study to demonstrate this, Anita Farel interviewed 212 mothers of kindergarten children from eight schools, half of them working mothers and half nonworking, and tested their children for persistence, creativity, curiosity, intelligence, consideration, and sociability.[8] As expected, children whose mothers were not working but who thought it would be better if they were did more poorly on almost all of these tests. Surprisingly, though, children whose mothers were working but thought they should not be working (another dissatisfied group) did not do more poorly on the tests. This may have been because the children were not exposed to as much of their mother's dissatisfaction, since she was away from them more, at work. It may have been because these children had special times with their mothers that compensated for the mother's dissatisfied caregiving. It may have been because the message conveyed by unhappy working mothers was basically accepting—that they wanted to be with the child more—while the message of the discontented full-time mother was more rejecting—that she would have liked more time away from the child by having a job. Or it may have been because mothers whose children were not developing as well wanted to spend less time with them. In any case, it is clear that neither the mother's attitudes and feelings about work nor her work status alone determined her child's development. How the child felt about himself and how well he developed were influenced by how his mother felt about herself and her roles as worker and mother, not simply by the fact that she worked.

One other possibility to explain the results of Farel's study is that the children of the dissatisfied working mothers who did not show the expected decrements in development were in daycare situations that compensated for their mother's dissatisfaction. Several other studies have shown that, when children are in very good daycare, their mother's behavior is likely to have less impact on their development than if the mother is the child's only caregiver.[9] Educational daycare can set up stimulating activities; a trained babysitter can choreograph intellectual experiences; a professional childminder can offer individualized attention, to compensate for lacks at home.

What about these other caregivers in daycare? Do we find the same effects of their behavior on children's development?

TEACHING STYLES

Like parents, teachers and other caregivers come in assorted sizes and shapes, and the behavior of the particular caregiver can make more difference to the child's experiences than simply the type of care arrangement provided.[10] In our discussion of daycare programs we have seen how the amount and kind of teacher control has a significant effect on children's behavior and development. When teachers in daycare are actively involved in stimulating children's thinking through talking, teaching, and providing interesting materials and a moderate number of educational tasks, this has clear benefits for the children's intellectual development and achievement. If the content of the stimulation includes social as well as intellectual skills, then children's cooperation and social behavior with peers may also be enhanced. Thus teachers, like mothers, can serve as verbal stimulators, providers of materials, and choreographers of intellectual experiences, and they often see it as their role to do so. When the teacher, sitter, or minder is responsive to the child's interests, goals, requests, and questions, it has been found that children are more independent, cooperative, and sociable. A caregiver can also provide or be the kind of social playmate the father is, perhaps with parallel benefits for children's sociability.

But what about the affection shown to the children in their charge by these caregivers? Is affection the exclusive province of parents? Does it matter if the teacher or caregiver is loving or rejecting? The answers from a number of studies seem to be no and yes. If a teacher creates a negative emotional climate in her classroom, this may cause children to learn less. On the other hand, if she is too physically demonstrative, this may distract children from their "work" and they will learn less. Caregivers who are warm and affectionate are likely to foster children's involvement in class activities, their sociability, happiness, security, helpfulness, and language—but they may not be so effective at getting children to do things they'd rather not.

As with parents, the caregiver's expression of affection or rejection is a backdrop for her managerial behaviors. One indication of how a teacher is combining emotion and discipline is her use of praise and criticism. Praise can be used effectively to manipulate children's behavior in the daycare setting. If they get praised for it, children will stay close to the caregiver, interact with her, or play with a child they would ordinarily have ignored; they will be more cooperative or aggressive, play with dolls rather than trucks, or persist longer at a particularly difficult task. But simply giving more praise in general does not make it more likely that children will learn and achieve more, concentrate on their work more, or work and play more independently or cooperatively (in fact, just the opposite has been found in some studies). It turns out that the kind of caregiver or teacher behavior that fosters these qualities in children's behavior, which makes them more positive, involved, cooperative, and facilitates more advanced play, is not the amount of praise or criticism, but the amount of encouragement from the teacher and the specific suggestions she makes. This is better for children's development than either the acceptance and affection implied by constant praise and permissiveness or the restriction that is involved in a critical, authoritarian style of management. Even if the authoritarian manner works for the time the child is with that caregiver (at least to the extent of behavior, if not intellectual advancement), as soon as the child escapes the oppressive regimen he may go wild and act out aggressively and disobediently. Thus we see there are clear parallels between the effects of parents and the effects of daycaregivers on children's development.

TRAINING AND EXPERIENCE

We have seen that knowledge about child development is related to mothers' behavior, and the same is true for other caregivers. With more training in child development, studies consistently find, preschool and daycare teachers and daycare home providers are more interactive, helpful, talkative, playful, positive, and affectionate with the children in their care (and the children are more involved, cooperative, persistent, and learn more).[11] For most teachers, though, there is still room for improvement in what they know about child development. In one study, fifty-three teachers from twenty daycare centers in Delaware were given a test to assess their knowledge of child development.[12] Most of them did quite poorly; on the average, these teachers got only slightly more than half of the questions correct.

Unlike specialized training in child development, neither general education nor the amount of experience in childcare is a very good predictor of caregivers' behavior. With no prior experience, there is a tendency for caregivers to simply go along with the child and not initiate any educational activities, and with more than ten years of experience, there is a tendency for teachers and caregivers to be stricter and more controlling.[13] But between these extremes there is no significant relation between experience and behavior, and even the relations at the extremes may be because caregivers with no experience versus those with over ten years of experience are two very different kinds of women (in age and career orientation); it is not that more experience necessarily makes a caregiver less accepting and permissive.

The sex of the caregiver does seem to make a definite difference in teaching styles and behaviors. Although both men and women teachers are likely to encourage what might be considered more feminine behaviors (sitting quietly, reading, painting, working on puzzles) in both boys and girls, male teachers are less likely to do this and, for boys at least, this has an advantage for their academic achievement.[14]

NUMBER AND CONSISTENCY

In policies for licensing daycare centers, the ratio of children to adults has commonly been used as a legislatible way of ensuring high-quality care. With more children per adult, it has been found that there is less caregiver-child contact of any kind; children spend more of their time playing with other children, in active physical games or make-believe play; they spend less time in intellectual activities (elaborated play, art, construction, work on puzzles and academic tasks); fewer of their questions are answered; conversations are shorter; and contact with the caregiver is more likely to involve prohibitions, commands, corrections, and routines. With too many children for one adult to attend to, children suffer and so do the staff—who are worn out at the end of the day.[15] Even so, the adult-child ratio is not as important in predicting how well children will do on developmental tests as is the sheer number of children present. With two teachers and twenty children, for example, children will do better if they are divided into two groups each with one teacher than if they stay in a single class with both teachers, even though both arrangements have the same adult-child ratio.

Another possible index of daycare quality is the length of time the caregivers have been in the daycare setting. Child development experts have decried the rapid turnover of personnel in daycare centers, the alacrity of daycare home providers to go out of business, and the tendency of babysitters to move on. They have been less vocal about "peer turnover" and the tendency of families themselves to change the child's care arrangement, but this also occurs with great frequency—possibly with similar results. Studies that have followed children over some period of time have found that approximately half of them have changed to a new care arrangement within one year, 30 percent within six months.[16] They are particularly likely to have changed care arrangements if they are over one year of age and if care was being provided by an unrelated, unlicensed sitter or minder who was young, inexperienced, and taking care of only one or two children. They are most likely to change from a home-care arrangement (babysitter, childminder, day-care home) to a center care arrangement (daycare center or nursery school).[17]

What kind of effect does this instability of daycare arrangements have on children's development? Two studies have shown that as a caregiver takes care of a child over a longer period of time, she forms a closer relationship with him (and possibly with his mother), and becomes more like the mother in her behavior (more affectionate, verbal, and responsive).[18] It might be expected that this would have benefits for the child. A study by Terence Moore in England tried to find out whether stable daycare was more beneficial than unstable care. In the study, six-year-old children who had more than two changes of care arrangement before they were five years old were found to be more insecure, fearful, and clingy and not to do as well on psychological tests as children in stable arrangements.[19] This conforms to other research showing that environments that are unstable because of changes in parents' work, health, or finances affect children's feelings of security and anxiety.[20]

But development is not always hindered by changing care arrangements. Another study found no difference in children's social competence related to the number of times they had changed daycare centers.[21] It may be that the detrimental effects observed by Moore were the result of other instabilities in the families of these children and not simply that they changed daycare arrangements more often. Experiencing interactions with more than one caregiver can have positive benefits, by providing variety and enrichment, by tempering of the effects of extreme caregiver styles, and by teaching the child to adapt to different caregivers. Change in itself is not necessarily detrimental for development, and staying with a poor caregiver is undoubtedly worse for the child than changing to a good one.

DIFFERENCES WITH PARENTS

The effect of teachers and caregivers on children's development may parallel the effects of parents, but a childminder is not the same as a mother; a daycare teacher is not just like daddy. Caregivers are unlikely to be as invested in their charges as parents are, and they do not have the same power to make important decisions. They usually have more training; they often have more experience; they are likely to be taking care of more children; and their care is always more open to scrutiny. But just how differently do they act?

A number of researchers have investigated this question. In one study, by Robert Hess and his associates, sixty-seven mothers of children attending daycare centers and thirty-four of their teachers were interviewed and observed interacting with the child in specified tasks.[22] When the adults were asked about their goals and expectations for young children, mothers and teachers agreed on many things: in valuing independence and social skills over academic abilities, for example. But teachers thought children's independence, emotional maturity, and expressiveness were more important than mothers did, and mothers thought politeness, social graces, and school skills more important than teachers did. These values went along with the disciplinary and management strategies each favored. Teachers appealed to rational rules and explanations; they were more flexible and permissive than mothers. Their requests were indirect and moderated ("Please put this block where it belongs." "I wonder how these blocks are alike. I wish you would tell me." "Can you tell me why you put that one there?"). They preferred to let children initiate actions rather than telling them how to do the task. Mothers, by contrast, were more direct, demanding, and task-oriented; they appealed to their own authority rather than abstract rules and made explicit corrections when the child made a mistake ("Put that block there." "Tell me why you put that block there." "No, put the other block there.").

The result of the Hess study in structured tasks in the laboratory are consistent with other studies comparing the behavior of mothers and daycare teachers in their natural habitats of home and center. Teachers are more permissive, more tolerant of disobedience and aggression, and less inclined to set standards. They justify their requests, explain their reasons, and help children find solutions. They join in play with the children and emphasize learning through play rather than only through formal lessons. Mothers tend to think these nursery school teachers are not strict enough, not sufficiently school-teacherish; they themselves are more authoritarian and demanding with their children. They talk more often and have more extended and far-ranging conversations. Their talk is likely to be social chatting, talk about do's and don't's, about past and future events, about what's happening at the moment. Children are more nearly equal participants in these conversations; they ask more questions and give more answers.[23] The different conversational styles of mothers and teachers are illustrated in the excerpts below, taken from transcripts made during observations of one four-year-old, Ann, playing at home and in nursery school.[24] At home:

> Ann: Come look at their little bit of hair.
> Mother: Love, I'm just looking for Ben's shorts. I don't know what he has done with them.
> Ann: Hum, look at his . . .Mum look at his little sh . . .look at his little h . . .Mummy, he's got a little bit hair, so come and have a look.
> Mother: Blue hair (laughs).
> Ann: What's wrong with blue hair?
> Mother: Well, I don't know, it can be fair hair, or brown hair, or red hair.
> Ann: Don't have red hair (indignant).
> Mother: Some people do. Know that boy in the park yesterday?
> Ann: Yea.
> Mother: With a kite.
> Ann: Yea, Mummy.
> Mother: He had what you call red hair, auburn. You know Daddy?
> Ann: Mm.
> Mother: He used to have red hair before it went grey.

And at nursery school:

> Teacher: What are you going to call your babies?
> Teacher: Hm?
> Teacher: What are you going to call your twins? Ann?
> Ann: Emily and Katy.
> Teacher: Emily . . .?
> Ann: And Katy.
> Teacher: Katy! Supposing they're boys? You can't call twins that if they're boys, can you? (laughs). (Ann laughs and goes off.)

Daycare home providers, childminders, and babysitters present another pattern of behavior in their interactions with children, one that is different from those of both nursery school or daycare center teachers and mothers, according to studies of this home daycare. Compared to teachers, they interact more with each child in one-to-one situations, especially when there is only one or at most two children, and they may be more positive and sensitive in their approach to the child. They also do more supervisory disciplining. Compared to mothers, they are cooler and more emotionally aloof, less playful and stimulating. They don't kiss or caress the children as often and are less tuned in to their individual interests.[25]

Although these generalizations about different patterns of behavior for mothers, teachers, and home daycaregivers are based on averages, which hide the enormous diversity found within each category of caregiver, they do suggest that in the child's life different kinds of caregivers are likely to play different kinds of roles. Mothers are likely to be loving and involved, salient and important, directive and effective; they give security, confidence, trust, and affection, exhibit strong emotions of love, joy, pain, and anger; they give specific socialization training (such as toilet training) and teach social rules and graces, moral norms and conventions, and conversational skills. Babysitters, childminders, and daycare home providers offer discipline and socialization without the emotional investment the parent feels and, building on the trust and confidence the child develops at home, provide the child with some variety and relief from the intensity of family interaction. Teachers in daycare centers and nursery schools foster the children's independence, self-sufficiency, and self-direction, providing formal education, intellectual knowledge, and opportunities for positive interaction with other children to increase the child's social competence.

8 / The Individual Child

Just as all caregivers are not alike, all children are not alike. Each one is a unique individual. There are limitations in how one can use the results of research, any research, in making decisions about any one child or situation. Research is based on statistical probabilities, not absolute truths. If a significant difference is found between groups of daycare and nondaycare children on a test, in one study or several, what this means is that children in daycare are *more likely* than children at home to behave in the way tested. It does not mean that every child who goes into daycare will in fact behave that way. Just as the weatherman can only predict a 70 percent chance of rain on a particular day, so research can only predict that, other things being equal, there is a greater probability that a child will behave in a certain way if he goes to daycare. Just as, even after hearing the weather forecast, each person has to decide for herself whether or not to take an umbrella, each parent has to decide whether or not to put any particular child in daycare. Research only gives the odds, no guarantees. Because research is based on the law of averages and ignores individual differences in order to present general conclusions, I have not been able to talk much about individual children in this book. Decisions about daycare for any individual child have to be made by individual parents, although knowing what happens to the "average child" should be helpful. Now I'll try to get a little more specific—although still bound by averages—by describing differences in daycare effects for different groups of children.

BOYS AND GIRLS

Researchers have documented scientifically what everyone has known all along, that boys and girls are different.[1] Even as young as two or three years of age, boys and girls act in ways that foreshadow their adult roles. Boys are more aggressive and competitive (especially with other boys), more physically energetic and assertive, and given a choice of toys go for bicycles, crates, cars, and guns, and play soccer and cops and robbers. Girls are more quiet and compliant, cooperative, friendly and compassionate, socially skilled and socially aware; they select dolls, dressups, and domestic toys, and play house. These differences show up in different countries. They persist even in the face of parents' conscious attempts to raise more socially responsible sons and more self-assertive daughters. They are patterns that children themselves are aware of by the time they are two years old.

What happens when boys and girls go to daycare? In daycare homes, caregivers act much the same as mothers do, in ways that permit or support these stereotypical patterns,[2] so no major change would be expected. But some people have suggested that attendance in a daycare center or nursery school reduces the stereotyped differences between boys and girls. This would be a reasonable expectation, since boys in daycare or nursery school programs have the opportunity and are encouraged to be sociable and to engage in quiet activities and girls have the opportunity and encouragement to be independent. But based on the available research, what seems to happen is that although boys in daycare do become more sociable than boys at home, and although girls in daycare do increase in autonomy, problem solving, and even belligerence over girls at home, this does not wipe out the differences between the sexes. Why not? Because, at the same time, boys in daycare also gain in independence and belligerence, and girls in daycare gain in social skills, over their home-reared peers; the sex-stereotyped differential remains. This may happen because in the daycare center, although teachers encourage both boys and girls to do quiet, academic tasks and discourage both boys and girls from aggression, they (and the other children) still tend to criticize girls for playing with boys and engaging in boyish activities and criticize boys for doing girlish things.[3] Even in daycare it is hard to get away from the sex roles that permeate our society.

INFANTS/TODDLERS/PRESCHOOLERS

Does it matter at what age a child begins daycare? Is there a best age to begin daycare?

In general, most evidence from all the studies that have looked for differences in daycare effects related to age indicates that such differences are relatively small and that there is no one best age for beginning daycare. Infants, placed in daycare in the first year of life, have been found in several studies to be more detached from their mothers, at the time.[4] But we don't know whether this is a permanent effect, since the same children were not observed at later ages. Children placed in daycare at two years may also be more detached from their mothers than those

starting later, but they have been found to adapt to daycare better than later starters, acting less withdrawn, dependent, defiant, or hostile.[5] In terms of cognitive gains
or achievement of social competence, age of starting daycare does not seem to matter; gains are evident after six to
twelve months in daycare, whether the child is two, three,
or four years old.[6] All in all, then, there is no strong evidence for daycare benefits or problems related to the
child's age.

EASY/DIFFICULT TEMPERAMENTS

"Difficult" babies cry intensely and often, spit out or
refuse new foods, sleep irregularly and briefly, and adapt
to change and new situations slowly, compared to "easy"
or "average" babies—and this difference in temperament
persists throughout childhood. Are there differences we
can predict in how difficult versus easy children will react
to daycare? Several researchers have studied how adjustment to daycare is related to individual children's temperaments. Craig Ramey and his colleagues followed infants from the time they were placed in the Frank Porter
Graham daycare center until they were three years old.[7]
In the first year of life, easy infants did better (in terms of
cognitive gains) than difficult ones, whether they were at
home or in the center, but easy infants did even better in
the center, while difficult ones did relatively worse. After
a year in this model daycare center, there was no longer a
difference in the effect of daycare on children of different
temperaments; both easy and difficult children were
learning more in the center. What temperament seems to
do is make the initial adjustment to daycare (a new and
complex situation) harder; difficult children do better

with a familiar, simpler caregiving situation, where they have more individualized care.

This need does not go away if the children start day-care when they are older. Joseph Marcus, Stella Chess, and Alexander Thomas studied older children who were entering nursery school.[8] Again, the initial adjustment was more problematic for children who had been identified as difficult or "slow to warm up" in infancy. But then the progress made by these children depended on the type of program they were in. In highly structured, formal, consistent, somewhat restrictive programs, easy children adapted readily; difficult children adapted eventually; slow-to-warm-up children withdrew; and extremely active or hyperactive children acted out. In open "laissez-faire" programs, easy children again adapted readily; slow-to-warm-up children adapted slowly; active children remained active but were not necessarily negative; and difficult children went on being difficult, giving frequent and irritating responses. Easy children thrive in any program—they are involved and happy, follow the rules, and get along with teachers and the other children. Other kinds of children need special care and consideration in the choice of a daycare program.

DIFFICULT HOME SITUATIONS

Some children are born with more difficult temperaments; others may have difficulties because they are born into families with problems. There may be money problems, divorce, violence, poor health, mental illness; these situations also make a difference in how children respond to daycare. Unfortunately, perhaps, it does not seem to happen that children from difficult home situations improve simply by getting away from the problem into a daycare arrangement. While it is true that children from low-income families gain from good daycare,[9] children from families with problems are still at a relative disadvantage, even in daycare. Within the same income level, children from families with fewer problems gain more from their daycare experience.[10] Children from homes disturbed by divorce, violence, neglect, or illness, who are unable to form close and secure, positive relationships with their parents, have been observed to be withdrawn and anxious, unable to leave their mothers to play with other children, less helpful and friendly with peers, less likely to interact positively with the caregiver, less likely or able to comply with adult rules in the daycare setting, and to have more difficulty adjusting to daycare.[11] Children from families wth problems have difficulties wherever they go. Daycare is no simple solution.

These unfortunate behaviors can be aggravated in daycare by a caregiver with little insight or warmth. Though it might be suggested that children from families with problems would do better in daycare homes than centers, since they could get more individual attention and there would be less stress and strangeness, this seems unlikely to be the case unless the daycare home provider is particularly supportive and sensitive. It could be argued just as plausibly that children from problem homes might do better in a busy, playful, cheerful nursery school which is very different from the home environment where the problems exist. It is impossible to say what kind of care arrangement would be most suitable for these children; the important thing probably is that they be given particular attention, care, and consideration wherever they are, or that they be placed in a particularly good daycare setting, whatever type it is, rather than expecting that day-care alone will alleviate the problems.

Finding the type of daycare arrangement and the particular setting that will be best for any individual child—boy or girl, toddler or preschooler, active or quiet, easy or difficult—is the inevitable challenge that faces the individual parent. How can a parent find and recognize a daycare setting of high quality?

9 / Quality

Given that a mother has made her decision to work, what type of childcare arrangement is best for her needs and the child's, how should she find it, how can she be sure that the particular facility she selects offers good care, and how can she increase the likelihood that her child will do well in the daycare setting? I'd like to offer some general and specific guidelines for telling good daycare centers or homes from bad, and some hints for ensuring continued high-quality care.

THE PARENTS' CHOICE

Parents decide whether they will use a babysitter, day-care home or daycare center by balancing three things: cost, convenience, and goals for the child. In the United States at least, at all income levels, the majority of parents prefer daycare in their own home, by a regular, nonrelated adult babysitter.[1] This arrangement is clearly most convenient, and with a babysitter they expect and usually find that they will be able to continue their control over the child's experiences and that the babysitter will respect their views and give the child the kind of discipline they agree with.[2] This, however, is usually the most costly kind of daycare. For that reason many parents choose daycare homes. Daycare homes may also be convenient, if close by, and they are flexible, familiar, and comfortable. Parents can still exert some control over their child's experiences, and daycare homes are the least expensive of all types of care.[3] If the parents' goals for the child are supervision, stimulating play, and school preparation,[4] they are most likely to choose the third alternative, a daycare center or nursery school. They give up some convenience to achieve these goals—especially if the program is only half day—but since costs run from relatively inexpensive to relatively expensive, they can often find one to fit their budget, especially if they are willing to be put on a waiting list until space is available.

Once a decision has been made about what type of daycare they want, parents usually look only for settings of that type. Their search usually proceeds first through an informal network of information sources: neighbors, friends, sisters. In one recent study by Douglas Powell of 611 households in Detroit, 89 percent of the women using regular daycare by a nonrelative had located the daycare setting this way.[5] Long-time friends were found to be the most helpful. A few of these women had used more formal or public means of searching—newspapers, telephone directories, bulletin boards, local childcare coordinating councils—after or instead of these informal sources, but they claimed these methods had not been very effective. Better, if friends failed, were local newsletters for finding babysitters, city social service departments for finding daycare homes, and just driving around for finding daycare centers. Only 15 percent of the women surveyed said it had been a problem to find daycare, but half of them claimed that they would have used an information-referral system if one had been available. Unfortunately, such systems are a rarity.

After a decision about the desired type of care has been made and one available setting or caregiver of that type has been located, the search usually stops. Most parents do not shop around; they are just glad to have found a place or person that will provide care for their child. A visit or phone call is all the checking up that is done. Children are often enrolled in centers, site unseen. The friends who have recommended the caregiver or center have not usually known more than a few caregivers or visited more than one center. A "professional" (doctor, professor) who might have made a recommendation has not usually visited any centers. Telephone directories do not screen listed daycare facilities for quality, and newspaper ads are clearly trying to sell their own places. Knowing that a center or a home is licensed indicates only that it meets certain minimal physical standards, not that it offers high-quality care. Community social service agencies are not allowed to give parents recommendations or evaluations about quality, even if they have them. A phone call to the daycare center or babysitter is not very informative about quality unless the caller asks very astute questions and gets very accurate answers. And even a visit to a setting can only give a general impression of the quality of care offered, unless the visitor observes systematically and compares observations made in several different facilities. Suggestions given in women's or parents' magazines about how to identify a center that provides good care are usually vague, untested, and hard to interpret and observe (how can the untrained parent know what "optimal amounts of touching, holding, smiling, and looking" are or what "balances interaction with leaving infant alone" means?).

For all these reasons most parents choose a particular daycare setting for the child on the basis of its physical conditions (clean, safe, good food) and their rapport with the daycare director or provider.[6] It is no suprise that in surveys of how satisfied parents are with the daycare their children are receiving, close to a third are not satisfied.[7] How can a parent become better informed about what good-quality care is and find out easily if a daycare center is providing it?

THE FEDERAL INTERAGENCY DAY CARE REQUIREMENTS

The Federal Interagency Day Care Requirements (FIDCR) are United States government standards for federally supported daycare facilities. They were finally agreed upon and endorsed by thirty childcare groups in 1980, after lengthy debate and research, but they have not yet been put into practice. Although these standards do not represent "ideal" daycare, they do provide a solid minimum for quality care. And while waiting for the government to enforce them, or for evaluating private centers that do not fall under their regulation,[8] parents might do well to adopt them as their own minimum standards. Very briefly, the FIDCR standards require these factors in a daycare setting.

- A planned daily program of developmentally appropriate activities which promotes the intellectual, social, emotional, and physical development of the children (for daycare centers, this should be written and available to parents; for daycare homes it need not be written).
- Trained caregivers with specialized training in childcare, who have also gone through an orientation that includes health, safety, and program procedures for that particular setting.
- Adequate and nutritious meals.
- A record of immunization for each child; information and help to parents about health services in the community.

- Opportunities for parents to observe the daycare setting and discuss the child's needs before enrollment; unlimited access to the setting to observe their child and regular opportunities to meet with the caregiver(s) to discuss the child's needs after enrollment; opportunity to participate in policy making for the setting; and access to evaluations or reports on the setting.
- The following staff-child ratios and group sizes:

	Age	*Maximum group size*	*Staff-child ratio*
For centers	0–2	6	1:3
	2–3	12	1:4
	3–6	16	1:8
For homes	0–2	10	1:5
	2–6	12	1:6

GUIDELINES FROM RESEARCH

A second way of deciding whether a daycare setting is providing high-quality care is to use the results of research such as that reviewed in this book. The following are some guidelines drawn from that research.

- In general, center-based programs (daycare centers and nursery schools) are more likely than home-based programs (babysitters, childminders, daycare homes) to provide educational opportunities for children and to increase their social competence, maturity, and intellectual development.
- In general, home-based care is more likely than center-based care to offer authoritative discipline, socialization training, and one-to-one adult-child interaction.
- Publicly funded daycare centers and nursery schools are the most likely kinds of group or center-based programs to offer care of high quality.
- Gains in children's achievement, positive attitude, intellectual development, and constructive play are most likely in programs (in homes or centers) that offer "a basic diet of free

choice punctuated by a moderate number of prescribed educational activities."

- Sociability, cooperation, and self-motivated exploration are most likely to develop in programs that are "open" and focus their efforts on free play and social interactions among the children in a rich and varied environment.

- High-quality experience is less likely in a crowded and disorganized space (with less than 25 square feet per child and no separated activity areas).

- An environment that offers a wide variety of materials and easy accessibility of things to do is ideal. Some of each of the following should be available: building construction materials (blocks, Legos); structured materials (puzzles, books); artistic materials (paints, musical instruments); manipulative materials (sand, buttons, water, dough, clay); social materials (games, cards, checkers, pickup sticks); fantasy or make-believe materials (dolls, dressups); active play equipment (slides, swings, tricycles); soft, cuddly materials (cushions, pillows, sofas).

- A daycare setting in which the child is part of a small group of children, both boys and girls, with an age range of about two years, offers more positive, cooperative, complex, and sustained interactions with both other children and the caregiver and has benefits for social development.

- The caregiver is the most important aspect of daycare. The caregiver-child ratio is not as important as the kinds of behavior the caregiver exhibits. Behavior that indicates high quality includes active involvement by talking, teaching, and playing; providing interesting materials; responding to the child's interest, advances, and questions; positive encouragement and suggestions; no demands, threats, or punishment. Although the caregiver is actively involved, she also permits the child freedom, initiative, and exploration; she is not restrictive or critical. High-quality caregiving in a daycare home or center is not indicated by an abundance of physical affection, constant praise, or strict discipline.

- A caregiver in either a home or a center who thinks of herself as a professional, has been trained in child development, has five to ten years of experience, and is part of a training and support network or educationally oriented centers is more likely to give this involved, active, positive care and to have a positive influence on the child's development.

• The best kind of care varies according to the individual needs of the child: for easy or average children, high quality is as described above; for slow-to-warm-up children, high-quality care would be slanted toward an unpressured, supportive atmosphere; for difficult children, toward more structure and consistency; active children need more latitude and less physical restrictiveness; withdrawn children may benefit from sensitive and nurturant caregiving in a busy, cheerful environment; insecure children may have trouble in any kind of daycare.

OBSERVATION CHECKLIST

A third and perhaps the best way of assessing the quality of a daycare setting is to make systematic observations in the facility. One checklist to guide such observations has been developed by Marilyn Bradbard and Richard Endsley.[9] These researchers took a list of items from the research literature and asked a panel of child development experts which items they thought best reflected good daycare. Then they field-tested the checklist by having mothers and college students observe in daycare centers that had been independently rated by experts. The checklist items that were found to differentiate between centers the experts had judged to be of high or low quality were put in a revised form of the checklist. These items did not include all the things about a daycare facility that might suggest its high quality; they were things that could be observed easily and reliably in a half-hour visit and that indicated important features of the quality of care. The Bradbard and Endsley checklist was designed for daycare centers only, but I am presenting a modified form of the checklist that applies to daycare homes and fits with the research-based guidelines listed above as well. There is no scale that goes along with the checklist to indicate when a center has achieved "high enough" quality status. The way to use the checklist is to fill it out for a number of daycare facilities and use their relative scores as an indication of their relative quality. This would then be an important factor in deliberations about which setting to use (along with cost, convenience, and goals).

Health and Safety
Adults do not smoke in the same room as children.
Floors are clean.
Floors are carpeted or have nonskid covering.
Children's eating area is clean and attractive.
No children with soiled diapers or pants.
At least one adult present at all times to supervise children.
Detergents, medicines, drugs kept out of reach of children (high shelf or locked cabinet).
Electrical outlets covered with safety caps.
First aid supplies (soap, bandaides, gauze, thermometer) available (ask).
Toys and equipment in good repair (no sharp edges, splinters, paint chips, electrical wires, loose parts on toys).
Heavy pieces of furniture (cabinets, bookcases) secure and stable, can't tip over on children.
Staff keeps records on each child (emergency phone numbers, medical information).
Woodworking or kitchen tools (hammers, scissors) and other sharp objects used only with adult supervision.

Physical Space
Individual space (locker, drawer, cubicle) for each child to store personal belongings.

Dark and quiet space to allow children to nap (shades or curtains can be closed, cots can be set up in separate area or there are bedrooms).

Storage space available for children to return toys and equipment to shelves after use.

Windows low enough for children to see outside.

Temperature and humidity comfortable (approximately 68–70 degrees F).

A variety of pictures, posters, mobiles in view.

Toileting area easy for children to get to.

Direct access to enclosed outdoor play area from the building.

Outdoor play area with open space for sunny days.

Outdoor play area with covered space for rainy days.

Outdoor play area easy to supervise (no hidden areas where children cannot be seen).

Outdoor play area well drained and covered with a soft surface (sand, bark, grass for tumbling, running, sitting) in one place and a hard surface (for riding toys) in another place.

Indoor play area with soft surfaces (pillows, cushions, rugs, easy chairs, couches).

Physical space not overcrowded (too many children, too much large equipment).

Materials, Equipment, and Activities

Attractive and well-written story and picture books.

Materials and equipment for quiet play (books, puzzles) and active play (riding toys, climbing structures).

Enough materials and equipment so that children do not have to wait more than a few minutes to use them.

Opportunities to run and climb both indoors and outdoors.

Choice of several activities (story, music, painting, puzzles) much of the time (except naps, meals time, lessons).

Full range of activities for both boys and girls (dressups, housekeeping, dolls for boys, climbing and riding toys, cars and trucks, tools for girls).

Both children and adults involved in cleaning up after activities (clearing table, folding laundry, putting away paints).

Some or all of the following materials: paints, crayons, pencils, paste, clay or dough, sand, water, scissors, paper, buttons.

Two or more of the following toys and equipment: riding toys, climbing equipment, pull toys, balance beam, pounding toys, stringing toys, nested boxes.

Two or more of the following toys and equipment: social games (checkers, pickup sticks), musical toys or instruments, toys or materials that teach the three R's (cards, puzzles, books).

Building or construction materials: wood, cardboard, boxes, blocks, tinkertoys, Legos.

In outdoor play area two or more of the following: blocks, cartons or boards for building, sandbox and sand toys, slides, riding toys, seesaw, balance beam, tires.

Play area indoors where no furniture or objects are off limits.

Toys and play materials accessible without asking (on low, open shelves, in toy chests).

Teachers, Adult Staff, and Caregivers

Enough adults to provide individual attention (probably at least 1 for every 6 children, more for children under 3 years).

Adults explain clearly what they want in words children can understand, often kneeling or bending over to the child's eye level when speaking.

Adults use encouragement, suggestion, and praise rather than orders, commands, prohibitions, criticism, or reprimands.

Adults respond to children's questions.

Adults are observed to teach children sometimes but not all the time (teaching may be informal, explaining, labeling, reading).

Some sort of educational program in evidence.

Adults have had some training in childcare and child development (ask).

Adults are interested in childcare as a career (attend meetings, read books, are part of a daycare network support, have ties to other community agencies), not just a temporary job (ask).

Adults do not spend all their time with one child while other children have nothing to do.

Male as well as female adults are employed by the center or available in the home.

No physical punishment.

Children

Children appear happy (laughing, joking) around adults.

Children are busy and involved (not wandering aimlessly, just sitting and staring blankly, waiting for a long time).

Each child spends some time interacting (playing, talking, working together) with other children.

Children seem to enjoy one another (help, smile, show approval, play).

No fighting (hitting, pinching, kicking, grabbing toys).

Children are in relatively small classes or groups in the center (no more than 18 preschoolers or 11 toddlers or 7 infants); in a daycare home, a small number of children attending (probably not more than 3).

Both boys and girls present.

Age spread of children is about 2 years.

Children are observed choosing a new activity on their own.

Parents

Staff encourages parents to visit any time.

Staff is willing to answer parents' questions or talk about the program.

Staff agrees with parent about discipline, child management.

Individual Child

Program is appropriate for particular needs and temperament of child (fill in for individual child).

ENSURING CONTINUED QUALITY

Selecting the setting, even after extensive and informed assessment and deliberation, is only the first step in the daycare saga. The parents' task is not yet done, and further steps are necessary to see that what looks like a care arrangement of high quality really turns out to be so.

Preparing the child. Before enrolling or leaving the child in the daycare facility, it is helpful to visit the setting together, to talk to the child about what it means and what to expect in daycare, and to give the child prior experience with other children (in a playgroup, for instance).

Easing the separation. Plunking the child down in daycare on day 1, with no warning, should be avoided. The immediate effects of leaving the child in the daycare setting or with the babysitter, which can be distressing if the child is young (up to three years) and is not used to separations from his mother, can be alleviated if not eliminated by providing a "security blanket" or favorite toy, the presence of some other family member (father, grandmother, sibling) or friend, by giving the child information about the mother's absence and expected return, by staying with the child until the setting and caregiver are familiar, and by progressively lengthening absences over the first week or two.[10]

Monitoring the child's progress. While the child is in any form of daycare, the parents should visit the facility periodically to check whether the child seems happy and involved; they should monitor his behavior and development at home, being vigilant for the occurrence of any new problems (tantrums, nightmares, bedwetting), comparing his developmental progress with that of other children the same age and checking that he is forming friends in the daycare setting and developing social skills.

Monitoring the caregiver's program. Even though the caregiver "passed the test" of giving good care to other children before the daycare setting was selected, what matters most is that she gives good care to the parents' own child after the selection is made. It is necessary for the parents to keep an eye on her behavior and talk things over with her regularly. Communication with the caregiver is difficult—in fact, it rarely occurs—but important nonetheless. The child should be the focus of regular, if not daily, conversation. The parent should encourage the caregiver to tell her what the child did that day and should inform her of his behavior and events at home. She should talk to the caregiver so that her goals and desires become explicit and so that she understands the caregiver's "hidden agenda" at the same time. If the daycare arrangement is out of the child's home, it might be valuable to invite the caregiver to visit the child at home. It could also be beneficial for the parent to get active in center activities: building up a library, being a guest, bringing cookies, just to keep the lines of communication open and to keep a concerned eye on caregiver and child.

Keeping the status quo. Stability and consistency of care is important for the child; too many changes can disrupt development. But if the parent or the child is unhappy with the arrangement, a change is preferable to continued irritation. Before the change, it is important again to ensure that the child be prepared and that the next setting or caregiver is more carefully screened.

Active advocacy for daycare. Finally, to improve the quality of daycare for all children, parents can become active advocates for daycare beyond their own immediate needs—joining parents' groups, lobbying, involving the media, schools, churches, and community organizations, speaking out for licensing, research, and new models of daycare, donating their toys, time, and materials.

Daycare is a fact of modern life, no longer a debatable issue. What is still open is how good the daycare available will be. Only by being informed and active, can parents and professionals help to ensure that daycare now and for continued generations of children will be the best our society can provide. For daycare is not only a problem for individual parents; it is a problem for society.

10 / Alternatives

In this book I have focused on daycare in the United States and Great Britain. It is clear that solutions to the problem of providing alternative care for children of working mothers in these two countries are makeshift at best. Now let us take a look at daycare in several other countries—France, Sweden, Russia, China, and Israel—to see the variety of solutions these societies have found in their pressing needs for daycare.[1]

FRANCE: CRECHES AND ECOLES MATERNELLES

Daycare began in France. In 1799, Johann Oberlin, a Protestant minister, was prodded by his maidservant, Louise Sheppler, into opening the first day nursery, in Alsace. It was a response to the plight of children left on their own while their mothers worked in the fields. The first crèche (infant day nursery) opened in Paris in 1844, again for the benefit of children whose mothers worked. Today in France daycare for children of working mothers is provided in crèches for infants from six weeks to three years and in écoles maternelles for children from three to six years. Fifteen percent of all infants are in crèches; 85 percent of all three-to-six-year-olds are in écoles maternelles. Both operate full day programs.

Crèches emphasize physical care, health, safety, cleanliness, and motor development and are staffed by "nurses" (after junior high school and two years of vocational training). Since there are not enough places available for all families who want them, priority is given to single parents or problem families. Crèches are government-approved and subsidized, but a fee on a sliding scale is charged. They are located in buildings with a courtyard or garden, and the crèche director has an apartment in the building. Each has forty to sixty children.

Écoles maternelles are like free nursery schools or kindergartens. They are basically educational, emphasize social and cognitive development, and are staffed by teachers. They are located near schools. They differ from nursery schools only in that they operate longer hours: from 9 to 12 (or 8 to 11) and 1 to 4, with a supervised meal period for children who can't go home for lunch.

SWEDEN: LEAVES AND DAGHEMS

In Sweden the government takes a particularly active role in providing services for all individuals, from birth to old age. The social security system covers childbirth, health, education, and family support. Childrearing is considered a responsibility to be shared by both parents and society. Consequently, the Swedish solution to the problem posed by working mothers includes lengthy paid maternity and paternity leaves, paid leaves for a parent when a child is sick, and a reduced work week for both parents. After the maternity or paternity leaves are over, daycare centers (daghems) provide care for children from six months to seven years, offering either full-or part-time care, whichever the parents want. These centers are of uniformly high quality, spacious, well-equipped, educational, and located in buildings specifically designed for that purpose. Their staffs include teachers, nurses, and instructors in childcare. Even in Sweden, however, since the proportion of women working is so high (over 65 percent), the demand for center spaces exceeds the supply, so licensed daycare homes are also used. Both these forms of daycare have expanded dramatically in the past 15 years. The number of places in licensed daycare facilities increased 700 percent from 1965 to 1970.

THE SOVIET UNION: BABUSHKAS AND YASLI-SADS

Like Sweden, the Soviet Union has a socialist family policy, which offers an extensive system of health care and social services. Since it is essential for the economy of the nation that mothers work, the Russians have instituted as part of this system the most extensive program of group upbringing in human history. Although mothers can take up to a year's maternity leave, they usually return to work much sooner. The Soviet daycare program encourages group care because of the communist notion that children are to be brought up "in the collective, by the collective, and for the collective." It was started with Khrushchev in 1956 and has become a highly centralized and sophisticated system of state-run yasli-sads (nurseries and kindergartens).

Children are still likely to be cared for by a babushka (grandmother) in their infancy, but, lacking a babushka, the state nurseries are available from six weeks on. By the time they are two or three, most children are in these nurseries; at four years they go to a state kindergarten. Statistics are hard to obtain, but it is estimated that there are 13 million children in fulltime care in these nurseries and kindergartens, ranging from 20 percent of the three- to seven-year-olds in rural areas to 75 percent of the three- to seven-year-olds in the cities. In Moscow there are 3000 yasli-sads.

The programs in these nurseries and kindergartens, both under the Ministry of Education, is the most highly developed and uniform in the world. The curriculum is based on early childhood research and emphasizes industriousness, aesthetics, character, cooperation, group awareness, problem solving, and creativity. Although there is time for children to indulge in role play, games of stimulation and physical exercise, gymnastics, and music, nothing is left to chance in this curriculum; everything is planned and specified—even the temperature—and spontaneous play only occurs at prescribed times and places, directed by nurse-upbringers who have three years' training at a teachers' college. Cooperation and helping are strongly encouraged: children are placed together in playpens at an early age, and all toys belong to the group, not individuals. The children learn early that "what's mine is ours, what's ours is mine." As soon as they can talk, children are also given training in evaluating and criticizing each other's behaviors from the point of view of the group.

The following excerpt from the manual that all nurse-upbringers follow illustrates the specificity of the curriculum.[2]

PLAY AND ACTIVITY: SECOND AND THIRD YEARS

Activity with spherical objects
   Goal: to acquaint children with the characteristics of spherical objects and basic colors.

A toy bowling alley (40 cm. long, 10 cm. wide, 15 cm. high, and with sides 2–3 cm. high) is used. Also a medium sized box which contains small wooden balls of 4 colors (red, blue, yellow, and green). There should be two balls of each color.

Procedure: Six children are seated in a semicircle, the adult facing them. The "bowling alley" is put in such a position that the balls roll toward the children. She shows how one rolls the balls. She says: "Children, I have some balls in my box. Look, how beautiful they are." She shows them red balls and places them into their hands. "I'll roll the red ball. It rolls this way. It rolled to Natasha. Natasha, please bring me the red ball. It rolled to Yura. Yura, please bring the red ball and put it in the box. Natasha, sit on your chair." In this way she shows blue, yellow, and green balls. Then she says: "Roll the yellow ball. Natasha, please bring me the yellow ball. Take the same ball and roll it in the 'bowling alley.' " The children bring the balls, take them out of the box and roll them.

CHINA: AUNTIES AND KINDERGARTENS

China also has an extensive system of nurseries, though it is less extensive than the Soviet Union's and differs considerably in content. For one thing, it is much more casual. The Russian upbringer has three years of professional school; the Chinese "auntie" may be chosen for childcare because she is patient and responsible; she is not likely to have completed high school. The Chinese nursery for infants up to age three is usually located in the factory so that the mother can come by to nurse her infant. Children are in small groups (six or seven) of same-age peers with one auntie. The youngest infants (two to eight months) are put in pairs in playpens or carriages; there is no attempt by the auntie to "stimulate" them. When they are old enough, the infants sit together in a circle and play group games, in an orderly manner, or perform songs and dances together. Infants are not encouraged to walk, crawl, play alone, or explore materials; their activities are social and artistic, not cognitive or academic. Their daily schedule is structured, not free-flowing.

After age three, the children go to kindergarten. Here there are toys and educational materials, but no science materials, table games, blocks, dramatic play props, or picture books as one might find in a Western nursery school or kindergarten. The curriculum consists of language and politics, mathematics, group recitation, song and dance, drawing and painting, physical training, and productive labor. There is no free choice or creative problem-solving activity. All activities are geared toward the goals of work and serving others.

ISRAEL: KIBBUTZIM AND METAPLOT

About three percent of the population of Israel live in kibbutzim. The kibbutz offers a very different childcare arrangement, also based on communal ideology and a national need for all citizens, including women, to work. In most kibbutzim the children live in a "Children's House" rather than with their own families. There they spend their time in a social unit of four or five other children of the same age, under the supervision of a metapelet. Each unit has its own bedroom, bathroom, dining room, playroom, and yard. At first, when the child is only a baby, the mother spends her time with him and the metapelet in the Infant House. But after the first year the child goes to the Toddler House and then to the Children's House. There he usually sees his parents and siblings only during the children's hour, two hours in the late afternoon when the family gets together in the parents' quarters. These visits with his parents are purely social; instruction, discipline, and physical caregiving are taken care of in the Children's House. Parents may visit the child at the Children's House at other times and are encouraged to do so for their own emotional satisfaction, but visits are supposed to be brief with no disruption of the child's routine. The parent can participate in the ongoing activity, but should not interfere with or comment about the work of the metapelet.

Metaplot are selected as teenagers after they demonstrate an aptitude for childcare by helping in the Children's House. They are trained and follow a manual that contains specific instructions for their work—including how to relate to the mother, how to toilet-train the child, what table manners to instill, and how to read stories.[3] They are solely responsible for dressing, supervising, and training "their" youngsters. When children are four to seven years old, the metapelet assists a teacher in giving a larger group of children lessons in science, art, and nature. Since it is believed that children must grow to depend on themselves, the metapelet encourages independence by leaving the children alone together for long periods.

The effects of this dramatically different form of child-rearing have been studied in Israel, by comparing the development of kibbutz children with that of other Israeli children raised in traditional families with greater participation in care by their parents (including children in a Moshav, a community with the same cooperative ideology but a traditional family structure).[4] These studies show no differences in mental development or mental health, but there are some differences in the qualities of the children's relationships with family and friends. Kibbutz children do form strong, positive relationships with their mothers, siblings, and friends, just as children in more traditional family arrangements do, but their feelings—both positive and negative—in the relationships are more moderate and not so focused on single individuals. They diffuse their affection across a larger number of people and have less deeply intimate relations with any of them. They see their parents as more nurturant and supportive but at the same time more encouraging of independence; their peers are seen as more supportive, but still their friendships are less intense. In addition to this difference in the intensity of interpersonal relations, kibbutz children are able earlier to approach and be sociable to unfamiliar children, to see another person's point of view, and to cooperate in group activities.

Some people have generalized from these apparent effects of kibbutz rearing to children in American daycare centers or British day nurseries, worrying that these children will lose their fondness for their families. But it should be stressed that the kibbutz involves a much greater degree of group rearing and parent-child separation than any fulltime daycare in these other countries.

RECOMMENDATIONS

Thus we see in this very quick and selective trip around the world a hint of the enormous variation that exists in daycare arrangements, programs, and systems. The need for daycare is felt everywhere. Yet in all these other countries we also see that more concerted efforts at the national level have been made to provide the needed facilities. We, too, should increase our efforts to provide the kinds of daycare that have been found in our own and these other countries to be most satisfactory. We might take from the policies in other countries, as well as from the results of research in our own, the following suggestions of possible ways to improve daycare in the United States, Canada, and Great Britain.

- Extend the length of day in existing nursery school arrangements (to make them more like the French écoles maternelles, for example).
- Extend the age of admission in daycare centers to include infants (as in the Swedish daghems) or set up infant and toddler facilities (like the French crèches, Soviet state nurseries, Chinese nurseries, and Israeli Infant and Toddler Houses).
- Encourage a more explicitly educational curriculum in daycare. Of course the curriculum in the United States, Canada, and Great Britain should be based on Western values stressing verbal skills, artistic expression, social competence, independence and free choice, not taken from the manuals for Soviet nurse-upbringers or Israeli metaplot. The idea of having a standardized curriculum as these countries do would probably never be accepted here, where diversity that allows parents options, and their children programs matched to individual needs, is stressed.
- Select daycaregivers on the basis of aptitude (like the Israeli metapelet or the Chinese auntie), then train them in child development (like the metapelet or the Soviet nurse-upbringer), and offer them ongoing consultation with expert advisers (like the Swedish childcare instructors).
- Integrate daycare into a larger system of childcare supports (such as the maternity leaves in Sweden and the Soviet Union).
- Have more systematic, if not centralized, supervision of daycare facilities (as in most of these countries).

- Include both center- and home-based daycare under such supervision, in networks of associated facilities.

If suggestions like these could be incorporated into day-care policy—informal as it now is in the United States, Canada, and Great Britain—working mothers, their children, and society would all be the beneficiaries.

References
Suggested Reading
Index

References

1 / The Problem

1. J. P. Robinson, J. Yerby, M. Fieweger, and N. Somerick, "Sex-Role Differences in Time Use," *Sex Roles*, 1977, *3*, 443-458. K. E. Walker and M. E. Woods, "Time Use for Care of Family Members," Use-of-Time Research Project, Human Ecology, Cornell University, Working Paper No. 1, September 1972.
2. For example, J. Curtis, *Working Mothers* (New York: Doubleday, 1976). E. Thomopoulos and H. M. Huyck, paper presented at the annual convention of the American Psychological Association, Washington, 1976. S. Welch and A. Booth, "Employment and Health among Married Woman with Children," *Sex Roles*, 1977, *3*, 385-397. L. W. Hoffman, "Effect of Maternal Employment on the Child," *Child Development*, 1961, *32*, 187-197.
3. J. E. Harrell and C. A. Ridley, "Substitute Child Care, Maternal Employment and the Quality of Mother-Child Interaction," *Journal of Marriage and the Family*, 1975, *37*, 556-564. M. R. Yarrow, P. Scott, L. DeLeeuw, and C. Heinig, "Child-Rearing in Families of Working and Nonworking Mothers," *Sociometry*, 1962, *25*, 122-140. Hoffman, "Effect of Maternal Employment on the Child." It should be noted that it is not possible to establish from these studies on samples in which it was the subject's own choice (not the researcher's) whether to work or not, whether the satisfied mothers would have been satisfied no matter what they were doing (working or not working)

2 / New Needs

1. S. L. Hofferth, "Day Care in the Next Decade: 1980-1990," *Journal of Marriage and the Family*, 1979, *41*, 649-658.
2. M. C. Howell, "Employed Mothers and Their Families (I)," *Pediatrics*, 1973, *52*, 252-263.
3. S. Yudkin and A. Holme, *Working Mothers and Their Children* (London: Sphere Books, 1969).
4. Hofferth, "Day Care in the Next Decade."
5. G. Russell, "The Father Role and Its Relation to Masculinity, Femininity, and Androgyny," *Child Development*, 1978, *49*, 1174-1181.

6. Reported in *Newsweek*, November 10, 1980, p. 110.
7. J. Kellerman and E. R. Katz, "Attitudes toward the Division of Child-Rearing Responsibilities," *Sex Roles, 1978,* 4, 505-512.
8. Walker and Woods, "Time Use for Care of Family Members."
9. H. H. Bohen and A. Viveros-Long, *Balancing Jobs and Family Life* (Philadelphia: Temple University Press, 1981).
10. Yankelovich, Skelly and White, Inc., *Raising Children in a Changing Society*, General Mills American Family Report, 1976-1977 (Minneapolis: General Mills, 1977), pp. 3-4.
11. K. Keniston and the Carnegie Council on Children, *All Our Children* (New York: Harcourt, Brace, Jovanovich, 1977).
12. G. W. Brown and T. O. Harris, *Social Origins of Depression* (London: Tavistock, 1978).
13. D. Belle et al., "The Impact of Stress on Mothers and Their Children," paper presented at the annual convention of the American Psychological Association, Toronto, August 1978.
14. Survey by the magazine *Family Circle* of 10,000 working women, 1978.
15. M. Bone, *Preschool Children and the Need for Day Care* (London: Her Majesty's Stationery Office, Office of Population Censuses and Surveys, Social Survey Division, 1977). Study of childcare arrangements by Thomas Coram Research Unit, London, 1977.
16. Bone, *Preschool Children and the Need for Day Care.* K. Dickinson, "Child Care," in G. J. Duncan and J. N. Morgan, eds., *Five Thousand American Families*, vol. 3, 1975, Survey Research Center, Institute for Social Research, University of Michigan, Ann Arbor.
17. S. Fraiberg, *Every Child's Birthright: In Defense of Mothering* (New York: Basic Books, 1977).
18. B. Spock, *Raising Children in a Difficult Time* (New York: W. W. Norton, 1974).
19. B. L. White, *The First Three Years of Life* (Englewood Cliffs, N.J.: Prentice Hall, 1975).
20. B. Bettelheim, "Should a Mother Feel Guilty About Wanting To Send Her Toddler to a Day-Care Center?" *Ladies Home Journal,* September 1971, pp. 34-35.
21. J. Kagan, "Day Care Given Clean Bill of Health," an interview in *APA Monitor*, December 1977.
22. B. Spock, *Baby and Child Care* (New York: Pocket Books, 1976). J. Kagan and P. Whitten, "Day Care Can Be Dangerous," *Psychology Today*, August 1970, pp. 36-39. J. Bowlby, *Child Care and the*

Growth of Love (Baltimore: Penguin, 1953), p. 60. R. Dinnage, "Understanding Loss: The Bowlby Canon," *Psychology Today*, May 1980, pp. 56-60.

23. K. A. Clarke-Stewart with N. Apfel, "Evaluating Parental Effects on Child Development," in L. S. Shulman, ed., *Review of Research in Education*, vol. 6 (Itasca, Ill.: F. E. Peacock, 1978).

3 / History

1. For documentation and more detail on the history of daycare in the United States, see M. O. Steinfels, *Who's Minding the Children? The History and Politics of Day Care in America* (New York: Simon and Schuster, 1973). N. M. Robinson, H. B. Robinson, M. A. Darling, and G. Holm, *A World of Children: Day Care and Preschool Institutions* (Monterey, Calif.: Brooks/Cole, 1979).

2. For more about the history of daycare in Great Britain see J. Tizard, P. Moss, and J. Perry, *All Our Children: Pre-School Services in a Changing Society* (London: Temple Smith, 1976). J. Bruner, *Under Five in Britain* (London: Grant McIntyre, 1980). W. Van der Eyken, *The Pre-School Years* (Hammondsworth: Penguin, 1977, 4th ed.).

4 / Here and Now

1. Dickinson, "Child Care."

2. M. D. Keyserling, *Windows on Day Care: A Report on the Findings of Members of the National Council of Jewish Women on Day Care Needs and Services in Their Communities* (Educational Resources Information Center [ERIC], 1972, ED 063 027). ERIC publications may be obtained from their Document Service, P.O. Box 190, Arlington, Virginia 22210.

3. For example, M. Golden et al., *The New York City Infant Day Care Study* (New York: Medical and Health Association of New York City, 1978). A. C. Emlen et al., *Child Care by Kith: A Study of the Family Day Care Relationships of Working Mothers and Neighborhood Caregivers* (ERIC, 1971, ED 060 955). S. Fosburg et al., *National Day Care Home Study* (Cambridge, Mass.: Abt Associates, 1980).

4. B. Jackson and S. Jackson, *Childminder* (London: Routledge and Kegan Paul, 1978).

5. For example, B. Bryant, M. Harris, and D. Newton, *Children and*

Minders (London: Grant McIntyre, 1980). B. Mayall and P. Petrie, *Minder, Mother, and Child* (London: University of London, Institute of Education, 1977).

6. Bryant et al., *Children and Minders*, pp. 114-115.

7. Ibid., pp. 154-155.

8. For example, Golden et al., *The New York City Infant Day Care Study*. B. Tyler and L. Dittmann, "Meeting the Toddler More than Halfway: The Behavior of Toddlers and Their Caregivers," *Young Children*, January 1980, p. 39. M. M. Cochran, "A Comparison of Group Day and Family Child-Rearing Patterns in Sweden," *Child Development*, 1977, 48, 702-707. E. Prescott, *Group and Family Day Care: A Comparative Assessment*, February 1972, ERIC, ED 060 945.

9. These statistics are for the United States, from C. Coelen, F. Glantz, and D. Calore, *Day Care Centers in the U.S., 1976-1977* (Cambridge, Mass.: Abt Associates, 1978), and Keyserling, *Windows on Day Care*. But figures for Great Britain from C. Garland and S. White, *Children and Day Nurseries* (London: Grant McIntyre, 1980) point in the same direction.

10. K. Sylva, C. Roy, and M. Painter, *Child Watching at Play Group and Nursery School* (London: Grant McIntyre, 1980).

5 / Child Development

1. At the Frank Porter Graham Center in North Carolina by C. Ramey, D. Farran, and associates, and the Milwaukee Project in Wisconsin by R. Heber and H. Garber.

2. Golden et al., *The New York Infant Day Care Study*. C. T. Ramey, D. MacPhee, and K. O. Yeates, "Preventing Developmental Retardation: A General Systems Model," in L. Bond and J. Joffe, eds., *Facilitating Infant and Early Childhood Development* (Hanover, N.H.: University Press of New England, in press). H. B. Robinson and N. M. Robinson, "Longitudinal Development of Very Young Children in a Comprehensive Day Care Program: The First Two Years," *Child Development*, 1971, 42, 1673-1683. K. Vroegh, "Infant Day Care: Some Research Findings," unpublished papers, Institute for Juvenile Research, Chicago, 1976 (ERIC, ED 145 968).

3. J. W. B. Douglas and J. M. Blomfield, *Children under Five* (London: Allen and Unwin, 1958). W. Fowler and N. Khan, *The Later Effects of Infant Group Care: A Follow Up Study* (Toronto: Ontario Institute

for Studies in Education, 1974). M. E. Keister, "The Good Life" for Infants and Toddlers (Washington, D.C.: National Association for the Education of Young Children, 1970).

4. Douglas and Blomfield, Children under Five. Keister, "The Good Life" for Infants and Toddlers. A. Doyle, "Infant Development in Day Care," Developmental Psychology, 1978, 11, 655-656. R. Berfenstam and I. William-Olsson, Early Child Care in Sweden (London: Gordon and Breach, 1973). L. D. Steinberg and C. Green, "Three Types of Day Care: Choices, Concerns, and Consequences," unpublished paper, University of California, Irvine, 1977.

5. M. V. Peaslee, "The Development of Competency in Two-Year-Old Infants in Day Care and Home Reared Environments," doctoral dissertation, Florida State University, 1976.

6. For example, A. Doyle and K. Somers, "The Effects of Group and Family Day Care on Infant Attachment Behaviours," Canadian Journal of Behavioural Science, 1978, 10, 38-45. C. T. Ramey and P. J. Mills, "Social and Intellectual Consequences of Day Care for High-Risk Infants," in R. A. Webb, ed., Social Development in Childhood: Day Care Programs and Research (Baltimore: Johns Hopkins University Press, 1977). Robinson and Robinson, "Longitudinal Development of Very Young Children in a Comprehensive Day Care Program." W. Fowler, Day Care and Its Effects on Early Development: A Study of Group and Home Care in Multi-Ethnic, Working-Class Families (Toronto: Ontario Institute for Studies in Education, 1978). Fowler and Khan, The Later Effects of Infant Group Care. Golden et al., The New York Infant Day Care Study. J. Kagan, R. B. Kearsley, and P. R. Zelazo, Infancy: Its Place in Human Development (Cambridge, Mass.: Harvard University Press, 1978). J. L. Rubenstein, C. Howes, and P. Boyle, "A Two-Year Follow-Up of Infants in Community Based Infant Day Care," Journal of Child Psychology and Psychiatry, 1981, 22, 209-218. K. A. Clarke-Stewart and G. Fein, "Programs for Young Children: Day Care and Early Education," in P. Mussen, M. Haith, and J. Campos, eds., Carmichael's Manual of Child Psychology (New York: Wiley, in press).

7. Steinberg and Green, "Three Types of Day Care."

8. H. Garber and R. Heber, "Modification of Predicted Cognitive Development in High-Risk Children through Early Intervention," paper presented at the meeting of the American Educational Research Association, Boston, April 1980 (published in Intelligence, 1980, 4, no. 3). Fowler, Day Care and Its Effects on Early Development.

Fowler and Khan, *The Later Effects of Infant Group Care*. J. R. Lally and A. S. Honig, "The Family Development Research Program," final report (OCD-CB-100) to the Office of Child Development, Department of Health, Education, and Welfare, April 1977.

9. For example, reviews by J. W. Swift, "Effects of Early Group Experience: The Nursery School and Day Nursery," in M. L. Hoffman and L. W. Hoffman, eds., *Review of Child Development Research* (New York: Russell Sage Foundation, 1964). Van der Eyken, *The Pre-School Years*.

10. I. Lazar et al., "The Persistence of Preschool Effects: A Long-Term Follow-Up of Fourteen Infant and Preschool Experiments," final report (18-76-07843) to the Administration on Children, Youth, and Families, Office of Human Development Services, Department of Health, Education, and Welfare, September 1977.

11. For example, Doyle, "Infant Development in Day Care." Golden et al., *The New York City Infant Day Care Study*. Vroegh, "Infant Day Care." M. M. Saunders and M. E. Keister, "Follow-Up Studies of Children Enrolled in a Group Day Care Program in Infancy," unpublished paper, Department of Child Development and Family Relations, University of North Carolina, Greensboro, 1979. Clarke-Stewart and Fein, "Programs for Young Children."

12. M. Golden et al., *The New York City Infant Day Care Study* (New York: Medical and Health Research Association of New York City, 1978).

13. K. A. Clarke-Stewart, "The Chicago Study of Child Care and Development," forthcoming.

14. C. W. Anderson, R. J. Nagle, W. A. Roberts, and J. W. Smith, "Attachment to Substitute Caregivers as a Function of Center Quality and Caregiver Involvement," *Child Development*, 1981, *52*, 53-61. H. N. Ricciuti, "Fear and the Development of Social Attachments in the First Year of Life," in M. Lewis and L. A. Rosenblum, eds., *The Origins of Fear* (New York: Wiley, 1974). E. M. Cummings, "Caregiver Stability and Day Care," *Developmental Psychology*, 1980, *61*, 31-37.

15. For example, Cummings, "Caregiver Stability and Day Care." Kagan, Kearsley, and Zelazo, *Infancy*. Bryant et al., *Children and Minders*. Ricciuti, "Fear and the Development of Social Attachments in the First Year of Life." D. C. Farran and C. T. Ramey, "Infant Day Care and Attachment Behaviors toward Mothers and Teachers," *Child Development*, 1977, *48*, 1112-1116.

16. Kagan, Kearsley, and Zelazo, *Infancy*. Cummings, "Caregiver Stability and Day Care." A. S. Ragozin, "Attachment Behavior of Day Care and Home-Reared Children in a Laboratory Setting," paper presented at the meeting of the Society for Research in Child Development, New Orleans, 1977.

17. For example, M. C. Blehar, "Mother-Child Interaction in Day-Care and Home-Reared Children," in R. A. Webb, ed., *Social Development in Childhood: Day-Care Programs and Research* (Baltimore: Johns Hopkins University Press, 1977). D. S. Moskowitz, J. C. Schwarz, and D. A. Corsini, "Initiating Day Care at Three Years of Age: Effects on Attachment," *Child Development*, 1977, *48*, 1271-1276. B. E. Vaughn, F. L. Gove, and B. Egeland, "The Relationship between Out-of-Home Care and the Quality of Infant-Mother Attachment in an Economically Disadvantaged Population," *Child Development*, 1980, *51*, 1203-1214. E. Hock, "Working and Nonworking Mothers and Their Infants: A Comparative Study Of Maternal Caregiving Characteristics and Infant Social Behavior," *Merrill-Palmer Quarterly*, 1980, *26*, 79-102. Clarke-Stewart and Fein, "Programs for Young Children."

18. For example, Ramey et al., "Preventing Developmental Retardation." Fowler and Khan, *The Later Effects of Infant Group Care*. Rubenstein, Howes, and Boyle, "A Two-Year Follow-Up of Infants in Community Based Day Care." Lally and Honig, "The Family Development Research Program." Clarke-Stewart and Fein, "Programs for Young Children."

19. For example, T. Moore, "Exclusive Early Mothering and Its Alternatives: The Outcomes to Adolescence," *Scandinavian Journal of Psychology*, 1975, *16*, 255-272. Lally and Honig, "The Family Development Research Program." Fowler, *Day Care and Its Effects on Early Development*. Fowler and Khan, *The Later Effects of Infant Group Care*. Cochran, "A Comparison of Group Day and Family Child-Rearing Patterns in Sweden." Clarke-Stewart and Fein, "Programs for Young Children."

20. Steinberg and Green, "Three Types of Day Care."

6 / Programs, Places, Peers

1. E. Ferri, "Combined Nursery Centres," *Concern* (National Children's Bureau), Autumn 1980, no. 37. B. Tizard, J. Philips, and I. Plewis, "Play in Pre-School Centers, II. Effects on Play of the

Child's Social Class and of the Educational Orientation of the Centre," *Journal of Child Psychology and Psychiatry,* 1976, *17,* 265-274.

2. For example, K. J. Connolly and P. K. Smith, "Experimental Studies of the Preschool Environment," *International Journal of Early Childhood,* 1978, *10,* 86-95. J. E. Johnson, J. Ershler, and C. Bell, "Play Behavior in a Discovery-Based and a Formal-Education Preschool Program," *Child Development,* 1980, *51,* 271-274. L. B. Miller and J. L. Dyer, "Four Preschool Programs: Their Dimensions and Effects," *Monographs of the Society for Research in Child Development,* 1975, *40* (5-6, Serial No. 162).

3. Sylva et al., *Child Watching at Play Group and Nursery School.*

4. Connolly and Smith, "Experimental Studies of the Preschool Environment."

5. Reviewed by R. S. Soar and R. M. Soar, "An Attempt To Identify Measures of Teacher Effectiveness from Four Studies," paper presented at the meeting of the American Educational Research Association, San Francisco, April 1976.

6. Miller and Dyer, "Four Preschool Programs."

7. E. Prescott and T. G. David, "Concept Paper on the Effects of the Physical Environment on Day Care," unpublished paper, Pacific Oaks College, Pasadena, Calif., July 1976.

8. W. Rohe and A. H. Patterson, "The Effects of Varied Levels of Resources and Density on Behavior in a Day Care Center," in D. H. Carson, ed., *Man-Environment Interactions* (New York: Halsted Press, 1975). Connolly and Smith, "Experimental Studies of the Preschool Environment."

9. Fosburg et al., *National Day Care Home Study.*

10. For example, Connolly and Smith, "Experimental Studies of the Preschool Environment." Prescott and David, "Concept Paper on the Effects of the Physical Environment on Day Care." C. Howes and J. L. Rubenstein, "Toddler Peer Behavior in Two Types of Day Care," *Infant Behavior and Development,* in press. Clarke-Stewart and Fein, "Programs for Young Children."

11. Prescott and David, "Concept Paper on the Effects of the Physical Environment on Day Care."

12. L. Espinosa, "An Ecological Study of Family Day Care," doctoral dissertation, University of Chicago, 1980. Prescott and David, "Concept Paper on the Effects of the Physical Environment on Day Care."

13. For example, R. Ruopp, J. Travers, F. Glantz, and C. Coelen, *Children at the Center*, Final Report of the National Day Care Study (Cambridge, Mass.: Abt Associates, 1979). K. A. Clarke-Stewart, "Interactions between Mothers and Their Young Children: Characteristics and Consequences," *Monographs of the Society for Research in Child Development*, 1973, *38*, (6-7, Serial No. 153). Golden et al., *The New York City Infant Day Care Study*. Clarke-Stewart and Fein, "Programs for Young Children."

14. Sylva et al., *Child Watching at Play Group and Nursery School*.

15. A. Doyle, J. Connolly, and L. -P. Rivest, "The Effects of Playmate Familiarity on the Social Interactions of Young Children," *Child Development*, 1980, *51*, 217-223. J. L. Rubenstein and C. Howes, "Caregiving and Infant Behavior in Day Care and in Homes," *Developmental Psychology*, 1979, *15*, 1-24. M. Lewis, G. Young, J. Brooks, and L. Michalson, "The Beginning of Friendship," in M. Lewis and L. A. Rosenblum, eds., *Friendship and Peer Relations* (New York: Wiley-Interscience, 1975).

16. J. M. T. Becker, "A Learning Analysis of the Development of Peer-Oriented Behavior in Nine-Month-Old Infants," *Developmental Psychology*, 1977, *13*, 481-491.

17. A. F. Lieberman, "Preschoolers' Competence with a Peer: Relations with Attachment and Peer Experience," *Child Development*, 1977, *48*, 1277-1287.

18. For example, Sylva et al., *Child Watching at Play Group and Nursery School*. Swift, "Effects of Early Group Experience."

19. C. Howes and J. Rubenstein, "Prediction of Infant Adaptation to Day Care," paper presented at International Conference on Infant Studies, New Haven, April 1980. Clarke-Stewart, "The Chicago Study of Child Care and Development."

20. Ruopp et al., *Children at the Center*.

21. Sylva et al., *Child Watching at Play Group and Nursery School*. Connolly and Smith, "Experimental Studies of the Preschool Environment."

22. S. B. Greenberg and L. F. Peck, "A Study of Pre-Schoolers' Spontaneous Social Interaction Patterns in Three Settings: All Female, All Male, and Coed," paper presented at the meeting of the American Educational Research Association, Chicago, 1974.

23. For example, E. K. Beller, "Infant Day Care: A Longitudinal Study," Office of Child Development (OCD-CB-310), 1974. Fosburg et al., *National Day Care Home Study*. W. W. Hartup, "Chil-

dren and Their Friends," in H. McGurk, ed., *Issues in Childhood Social Development* (London: Methuen, 1978). Clarke-Stewart and Fein, "Programs for Young Children."

7 / Caregivers

1. See the general review by Clarke-Stewart and Apfel, "Evaluating Parental Effects on Child Development," for documentation.
2. F. Pedersen, R. Cain, M. Zaslow, and B. Anderson, "Variation in Infant Experience Associated with Alternative Family Role Organization," paper presented at the International Conference on Infancy Studies, New Haven, April 1980.
3. Hock, "Working and Nonworking Mothers and Their infants." S. E. Cohen, "Maternal Employment and Mother-Child Interaction," *Merrill-Palmer Quarterly*, 1978, 24, 189-197. J. B. Schubert, S. Bradley-Johnson, and J. Nuttall, "Mother-Infant Communication and Maternal Employment," *Child Development*, 1980, 51, 246-249.
4. Harrell and Ridley, "Substitute Child Care, Maternal Employment and the Quality of Mother-Child Interaction." Yarrow et al., "Child-Rearing in Families of Working and Nonworking Mothers." Hoffman, "Effect of Maternal Employment on the Child."
5. E. Hock, "Alternative Approaches to Child Rearing and Their Effects on the Mother-Infant Relationship," report (OCD-CB-490) to the Office of Child Development, Department of Health, Education, and Welfare, 1976. E. Hock and J. B. Clinger, "Behavior toward Mother and Stranger of Infants Who Have Experienced Group Day Care, Individual Day Care, or Exclusive Maternal Care," *Journal of Genetic Psychology*, 1980, 137, 49-61.
6. Schubert et al., "Mother-Infant Communication and Maternal Employment."
7. L. W. Hoffman, "Effects of Maternal Employment on the Child—A Review of the Research," *Developmental Psychology*, 1974, 10, 204-228.
8. A. M. Farel, "Effects of Preferred Maternal Roles, Maternal Employment, and Sociodemographic Status on School Adjustment and Competence," *Child Development*, 1980, 51, 1179-1186.
9. For example, Ramey et al., "Preventing Developmental Retardation: A General Systems Model."
10. For example, Soar and Soar, "An Attempt To Identify Measures

of Teacher Effectiveness from Four Studies." J. Carew, "Experience and the Development of Intelligence in Young Children," *Monographs of the Society for Research in Child Development*, 1980, 45, (1-2, Serial No. 183). B. I. Fagot, "Influence of Teacher Behavior in the Preschool," *Developmental Psychology*, 1973, 9, 198-206. Golden et al., *The New York City Infant Day Care Study*. J. Stallings, "Implementation and Child Effects of Teaching Practice in Follow-Through Classrooms," *Monographs of the Society for Research in Child Development*, 1975, 40 (3, Serial No. 163). Rubenstein and Howes, "Caregiving and Infant Behavior in Day Care and in Homes."

11. Tyler and Dittman, "Meeting the Toddler More than Halfway." Lazar et al., "The Persistence of Preschool Effects." Fosburg et al., "National Day Care Home Study." Espinosa, "An Ecological Study of Family Day Care." D. G. Klinzing and D. R. Klinzing, "An Examination of the Verbal Behavior, Knowledge, and Attitudes of Day Care Teachers," *Education*, 1974, 95, 65-71.

12. Klinzing and Klinzing, "An Examination of the Verbal Behavior, Knowledge, and Attitudes of Day Care Teachers."

13. Lazar et al., "The Persistence of Preschool Effects." Ruopp et al., *Children at the Center*. Fosburg et al., *National Day Care Home Study*. T. W. Jambor, "Teacher Role Behavior: Day Care Versus Nursery School," *Child Care Quarterly*, 1975, 4, 93-100. B. I. Fagot, "Reinforcing Contingencies for Sex-Role Behaviors: Effect of Experience with Children," *Child Development*, 1978, 49, 30-36.

14. For example, D. Gold, M. Reis, and C. Berger, "Male Teachers and the Development of Nursery School Children," *Psychological Reports*, 1979, 44, 457-458.

15. Connolly and Smith, "Experimental Studies of the Preschool Environment." Ruopp et al., *Children at the Center*. Sylva et al., *Child Watching at Play Group and Nursery School*. Lazar et al., "The Persistence of Preschool Effects." Golden et al., *The New York City Infant Day Care Study*.

16. S. Ambron, "Day Care and Early Social Development," unpublished paper, Boys Town Center for the Study of Youth Development, Stanford University, 1980. Emlen et al., *Child Care by Kith*. Clarke-Stewart, "The Chicago Study of Child Care and Development." Bryant et al., *Children and Minders*.

17. Clarke-Stewart, "The Chicago Study of Child Care and Development." Fosburg et al., *National Day Care Home Study*. Steinberg and Green, "Three Types of Day Care."

18. Cummings, "Caregiver Stability and Day Care." J. L. Rubenstein, F. A. Pedersen, and L. J. Yarrow, "What Happens When Mother Is Away: A Comparison of Mothers and Substitute Caregivers," *Developmental Psychology*, 1977, *13*, 529-530.
19. T. W. Moore, "Effects on the Children," in S. Yudkin and A. Holme, eds., *Working Mothers and Their Children* (London: Sphere Books, 1969).
20. For example, B. Vaughn, B. Egeland, and L. A. Sroufe, "Individual Differences in Infant-Mother Attachment at Twelve and Eighteen Months: Stability and Change in Families Under Stress," *Child Development*, 1979, *50*, 971-975.
21. R. R. Largman, "The Social-Emotional Effects of Age of Entry into Full-Time Group Care," doctoral dissertation, University of California, Berkeley, 1976.
22. R. D. Hess, G. C. Price, W. P. Dickson, and M. Conroy, "Different Roles for Mothers and Teachers: Contrasting Styles of Child Care," in S. Kilmer, ed., *Advances in Early Education and Day Care* (Greenwich, Conn.: JAI Press, 1980).
23. Rubenstein and Howes, "Caregiving and Infant Behavior in Day Care and in Homes." B. Tizard, H. Carmichael, M. Hughes, and G. Pinkerton, "Four Year Olds Talking to Mothers and Teachers," in L. A. Hersoveval, ed., *Language and Language Disorders in Childhood*, Supplement No. 2, *Journal of Child Psychology and Psychiatry* (London: Pergamon Press, 1980). Cochran, "A Comparison of Group Day and Family Child-Rearing Patterns in Sweden." C. S. Winetsky, "Comparison of the Expectations of Parents and Teachers for the Behavior of Preschool Children," *Child Development*, 1978, *49*, 1146-1154.
24. Tizard et al., "Four Year Olds Talking to Mothers and Teachers."
25. Cochran, "A Comparison of Group and Family Child-Rearing Patterns in Sweden." Clarke-Stewart, "The Chicago Study of Child Care and Development." Rubenstein et al., "What Happens When Mother Is Away." Bryant et al., *Children and Minders*.

8 / The Individual Child

1. For example, E. E. Maccoby and C. N. Jacklin, *The Psychology of Sex Differences* (Stanford, Calif.: Stanford University Press, 1974).
2. Cochran, "A Comparison of Group and Family-Rearing Patterns in Sweden."

3. R. L. Wynn, "The Effect of a Playmate on Day-Care and Home-Reared Toddlers in a Strange Situation," paper presented at the meeting of the Society for Research in Child Development, San Fransisco, March 1979. Fowler and Khan, *The Later Effects of Infant Group Care*. Moore, "Effects on the Children." L. O. Gunnarsson, "Children in Day Care and Family Care In Sweden: A Follow-up," doctoral dissertation, University of Michigan, 1978. B. I. Fagot, "Consequences of Moderate Cross-Gender Behavior in Preschool Children," *Child Development*, 1977, *48*, 902-907. P. K. Smith and M. Green, "Aggressive Behavior in English Nurseries and Play Groups: Sex Differences and Response of Adults," *Child Development*, 1975, *46*, 211-214. L. Bourdeau and T. J. Ryan, "Teacher Interaction with Preschool Children: Attitudes, Contacts, and Their Effects," *Canadian Journal of Behavioral Science*, 1978, *10*, 283-295.
4. P. M. Schwartz, "Length of Daily Separation Due to Child Care and Attachment Behaviors of 18 Month Old Infants," submitted for publication, 1980. Vaughn et al., "Individual Differences in Infant-Mother Attachment at Twelve and Eighteen Months." Hock, "Working and Nonworking Mothers and Their Infants."
5. Blehar, "Mother-Child Interaction in Day-Care and Home-Reared Children." Bryant et al., *Children and Minders*. Largman, "The Social-Emotional Effects of Age of Entry into Full-Time Group Care."
6. Golden et al., *The New York City Infant Day Care Study*. Robinson and Robinson, "Longitudinal Development of Very Young Children in a Comprehensive Day Care Program." Clarke-Stewart, "The Chicago Study of Child Care and Development." Ruopp et al., *Children at the Center*. Ferri, "Combined Nursery Centres."
7. Ramey et al., "Preventing Developmental Retardation."
8. J. Marcus, S. Chess, and A. Thomas, "Temperamental Individuality in Group Care of Young Children," *Early Child Development and Care*, 1972, *1*, 313-330.
9. Robinson and Robinson, "Longitudinal Development of Very Young Children in a Comprehensive Day Care Program."
10. Garber and Herber, "Modification of Predicted Cognitive Development in High-Risk Children through Early Intervention." Cochran, "A Comparison of Group and Family Child-Rearing Patterns in Sweden."

11. Bryant et al., *Children and Minders*. Howes and Rubenstein, "Prediction of Infant Adaptation to Day Care." R. P. Klein and J. T. Durfee, "Prediction of Preschool Social Behavior from Social-Emotional Development at One Year," *Child Psychiatry and Human Development*, 1979, *9*, 145-151. M. A. Easterbrooks and M. E. Lamb, "The Relationship between Quality of Infant-Mother Attachment and Infant Competence in Initial Encounters with Peers," *Child Development*, 1979, *50*, 380-387.

9 / Quality

1. J. Frost and H. Schneider, *Types of Day Care and Parents' Preferences*, Final Report: Part VII (ERIC, 1971, ED 068 195). C. R. Hill, *The Child Care Market: A Review of the Evidence and Implications for Federal Policy* (ERIC 1977, ED 156 352). Dickinson, *Child Care*. Emlen et al., *Child Care by Kith*.
2. Steinberg and Green, "Three Types of Day Care." S. Low and P. G. Spindler, "Child Care Arrangements of Working Mothers in the United States," U.S. Children's Bureau and U.S. Women's Bureau, 1968. F. A. Ruderman, *Child Care and Working Mothers: A Study of Arrangements Made for Daytime Care of Children* (New York: Child Welfare League of America, 1963).
3. Emlen et al., *Child Care by Kith*.
4. Ruopp et al., *Children at the Center*. Ruderman, *Child Care and Working Mothers*.
5. D. R. Powell, with J. W. Eisenstadt, "Finding Child Care: A Study of Parents' Search Processes," report for the Ford Foundation (780-0372), June 1980.
6. Powell and Eisenstadt, "Finding Child Care." M. R. Bradbard and R. C. Endsley, "What Do Licensers Say to Parents Who Ask Their Help with Selecting Quality Day Care?" *Child Care Quarterly*, 1979, *8*, 307-312. S. Auerbach-Fink, "Mothers' Expectations of Child Care," *Young Children*, 1977, *32*, 12-21.
7. Bone, *Preschool Children and the Need for Day Care*. Ruderman, *Child Care and Working Mothers*. Frost and Schneider, *Types of Day Care and Parents' Preferences*. Steinberg and Green, "Three Types of Day Care." E. Handler and J. Fredlund, *Differences between Highly Satisfied and Not Highly Satisfied Clients of Day Care Centers* (ERIC, 1971, ED 068 165).
8. According to the Department of Health, Education, and Welfare,

only about half of these private centers in 1980 met FIDCR standards.

9. Bradbard and Endsley, "What Do Licensers Say to Parents Who Ask Their Help with Selecting Quality Day Care?"

10. R. H. Passman, "Mothers and Blankets as Agents for Promoting Play and Exploration by Young Children in a Novel Environment: The Effects of Social and Nonsocial Attachment Objects," *Developmental Psychology*, 1975, *11*, 170-177. N. G. Blurton-Jones and G. Leach, "Behavior of Children and Their Mothers at Separation and Greeting," in N. G. Blurton-Jones, ed., *Ethological Studies of Child Behavior* (Cambridge, Eng.: Cambridge University Press, 1972). M. Kotelchuck, P. R. Zelazo, J. Kagan, and E. Spelke, "Infant Reactions to Parental Separations When Left with Familiar and Unfamiliar Adults," *Journal of Genetic Psychology*, 1975, *126*, 255-262. C. M. Heinicke and I. Westheimer, *Brief Separations* (New York: International Universities Press, 1965). M. Weinraub and M. Lewis, "The Determinants of Children's Responses to Separation," *Monographs of the Society for Research in Child Development*, 1977, *42* (4, Serial No. 172). J. C. Schwarz and R. Wynn, "The Effects of Mother's Presence and Previsits on Children's Emotional Reaction to Starting Nursery School," *Child Development*, 1971, *42*, 871-881.

10 / Alternatives

1. More about daycare in these and other countries can be found in U. Bronfenbrenner, *Two Worlds of Childhood: U.S. and U.S.S.R.* (New York: Basic Books, 1970). W. Kessen, *Childhood in China* (New Haven: Yale University Press, 1975). Robinson et al., *A World of Children: Day Care and Preschool Institutions*.

2. N. B. Kupriyanova and T. N. Fedoseeva, "Play and Activity for Children in the First Three Years of Life," cited in J. Marcus, ed., *Growing Up in Groups: The Russian Day Care Center and the Israeli Kibbutz: Two Manuals on Early Childcare* (New York: Gordon and Breach, 1972).

3. Y. Ben-Yaakov, "Methods of Kibbutz Collective Education during Early Childhood," cited in Marcus, *Growing Up in Groups.*

4. For example, B. Beit-Hallahmi and A. I. Rabin, "The Kibbutz as a Social Experiment and as a Child-Rearing Laboratory," *American Psychologist*, 1977, *32*, 532-541. A. Avgar, U. Bronfenbrenner, and

C. R. Henderson, "Socialization Practices of Parents, Teachers, and Peers in Israel: Kibbutz, Moshav, and City," *Child Development*, 1977, *48*, 1219-1227. H. T. Nahir and R. S. Yussen, "The Performance of Kibbutz- and City-Reared Israeli Children on Two Role-Taking Tasks," *Developmental Psychology*, 1977, *13*, 450-455. E. Regev, B. Beit-Hallahmi, and R. Sharabany, "Affective Expression in Kibbutz-Communal, Kibbutz-Familial, and City-Raised Children in Israel," *Child Development*, 1980, *51*, 232-237.

Suggested Reading

Jerome Bruner, *Under Five in Britain* (London: Grant McIntyre, or Ypsilanti, Mich.: High/Scope Press, 1980). An integrative and thoughtful overview of the methods and findings of the Oxford Preschool Research Project, a study that involved extensive and intensive observations and interviews at day nurseries, daycare centers, nursery schools, playgroups, and childminders' homes in Great Britain. More detailed information about different parts of the study can be found in other books in this series: Kathy Sylva, Carolyn Roy, and Marjorie Painter, *Child Watching at Playgroup and Nursery School*; Bridget Bryant, Miriam Harris, and Dee Newton, *Children and Minders*; Teresa Smith, *Parents and Preschool*; and Caroline Garland and Stephanie White, *Children and Day Nurseries*; all published by the same publishers in 1980.

Richard Endsley and Marilyn Bradbard, *Quality Day Care. A Handbook of Choices for Parents and Caregivers* (Englewood Cliffs, N.J.: Prentice-Hall, 1981). A useful guide to parents who are choosing among available daycare facilities.

Greta Fein and Alison Clarke-Stewart, *Day Care in Context* (New York: Wiley, 1973). A little out of date now but still provides useful background for the larger issues surrounding daycare (education, child development, politics).

Ellen Galinsky, and William Hooks, *The New Extended Family: Day Care That Works* (Boston: Houghton-Mifflin, 1977). Describes in pleasing detail a number of exemplary daycare facilities that illustrate the range of possible forms of good daycare.

Sally Kilmer, *Advances in Early Education and Daycare* (Greenwich, Conn.: JAI Press, 1980). First in a series of books (the others are in press or preparation) that will keep the reader up to date about current research.

Halbert B. Robinson, Nancy M. Robinson, Martin Wolins, Urie Bronfenbrenner, and Julius Richmond, *Early Child Care in the United States of America* (London: Gordon and Breach, 1973). One of a series of parallel books on day-care services, each dealing with a different country: Sweden, France, Switzerland, Cuba, Great Britain, Hungary, India, Poland, Israel, and the Soviet Union.

Nancy M. Robinson, Halbert B. Robinson, M. A. Darling, and G. Holm, *A World of Children: Day Care and Preschool Institutions* (Monterey, Calif.: Brooks/Cole, 1979). Daycare in an international context.

Jack Tizard, Peter Moss, and Jane Perry, *All Our Children. Preschool Services in a Changing Society* (London: Temple Smith/New Society, 1976). Describes the history and politics of daycare and other preschool services in Great Britain.

William Van der Eyken. *The Preschool Years*, 4th ed. (Harmondsworth: Penguin, 1977). Another good account of British daycare.

Index